Soulful Horsemanship

A Path to Emotional Freedom for the Horse and Human

Stef P. Durham

Second Edition Copyright © 2014 Stef Durham

First Edition Copyright © 2013 Stef Perkins

ISBN 978-1499114683

All rights reserved. No part of this publication may be reproduced, stored in a retrieval system, or transmitted in any form or by any means, electronic, mechanical, recording, or otherwise, without the prior written permission of the author. To obtain permission for reprints or excerpts please contact: stefdurham@soulfulyou.com

Disclaimer: All horse-related activities involve risk. The material in this book is made available on the understanding that readers exercise their own skill and care with respect to its use. Before relying on the material in any important matter, readers should carefully evaluate the accuracy, completeness, and relevance of the information, and should obtain appropriate professional advice related to their particular circumstances. Any application of the techniques, ideas, and suggestions from the author Stef Durham is at the reader's sole discretion and risk. The author does not guarantee the accuracy or completeness of any information published herein and is not responsible for any errors, omissions, or for the consequences resulting from the use of such information.

Further, the author accepts no liability or responsibility to any person or entity for any errors contained in this publication, or for any physical, emotional, or financial consequences or any special, incidental, or consequential damage caused or alleged to be caused directly or indirectly by the information contained in this book.

Printed in the United States of America

Stef Durham
Living Soulful, LLC
www.soulfulyou.com
Bend, OR
2014

Second Edition

*This book is dedicated to
Thelma and Snooks.
You are both a light in my life
And an inspiration.
Thank you for all of your
Love and caring over the years.
I love you both
With all my heart.*

Acknowledgments

I owe you, Jen, a HUGE thank you for your endless time, effort, and skill reading and editing all of the manuscripts of Soulful Horsemanship. This book would be a frightful mess if not for your love and dedication. I am so grateful to have you as my best friend. I love you so very much. Oh, and, I *commend* you!

Thanks to my Mom for everything. You are my number one cheerleader and supporter. I wouldn't get anywhere if it were not for your fearless belief in all my crazy ideas. You are my angel.

Thanks to my Dad for helping when I need it most. Your honesty last summer inspired me to speak my truth. You helped me find the courage to open my heart. I hope I can pass that gift on to others through this book and my work.

I wish to thank Jason for supporting me in everything I do. I am so appreciative for all of the hours you have listened to the re-writes of these pages. Your patience, kindness, and love are more than I could have ever dreamed.

Many thanks to my friends, family, teachers, students, and readers for encouraging me on my path. I do this work for all of us and I hope you get as much joy from it as I do.

Thanks to all of the horses who have touched my life. I would not be who I am today if it were not for the gifts that each bestowed upon me. I am so blessed to have these amazing teachers in my life.

Table of Contents

Introduction: Stef's Story 1

One: Empowered Partnership 5

    The vision 6

    Growth opportunities for humanity 11

    How do we relate to horses? 14

    A shift in partnership 19

    A new way to interact 23

    Making the choice to change 28

Two: Transformed Perspective 33

    Creating a safe environment 34

    Building your foundation 37

    How is Soulful Horsemanship different? 40

    Building a partnership 44

    The Soulful Horsemanship Pyramid 48

    Spiritual development in the barn 49

    Creative problem solving to benefit training 55

Three: Compassionate Confidence 63

    Shifting from fear to love 64

    Allowing authenticity 69

    Going back to basics 73

    Fostering partnership through play 79

    A change in dynamics: from ground work to riding 82

    Building confidence in the horse 86

Four: Intuitive Awareness 93

    Embracing emotion 94

    Mind, body, and heart 96

    Working with the horse to deepen your emotional awareness 101

    Mindful awareness 104

    Challenging emotions 107

    Following your intuition 113

    Staying present with patience 115

Five: Intentional Communication 123

    The need for a common language 123

    Exploration of communication on the ground 128

    Translating groundwork to the ridden aids 134

    Communicating rewards and corrections 141

    Practicing new communication skills 144

Six: Humble Leadership 155

    The dynamics of leadership 155

    Horses can teach us leadership skills 157

    Teaching your horse to read and write 163

    Managing misunderstandings 169

    Shaping the outcome 172

    Considerations for setting up a successful training session 176

Seven: Joyful Purpose 183

    You have a unique purpose 184

    The horse's purpose 188

    Searching for meaning 190

    The expression of purpose through partnership 195

    Conclusion 205

Soulful Horsemanship

Soulful: *full of or expressing deep feeling*
Horsemanship: *the art, ability, skill or manner of a horseman*

Introduction:
Stef's Story

I want to share with you the wisdom that I have gained from horses through my journey. I have faced a number of issues in my life, just like you. We all have our challenges but it is through the lessons that we learn from those difficult bits of life that we can find our own power and authenticity. My path has been about shifting from fear to empowerment; from self-doubt to self-love; from wearing masks to living with integrity; and from chasing money to living from the heart.

The one constant in my life was always horses. Truthfully, I had no natural talent and was terrified before every lesson because my instructor just might ask me to do something I wasn't comfortable with. Despite my fear I continued to ride, compete, and work with horses because I loved them. I could be myself in those quiet moments mucking stalls or grooming. So I continued to learn and push myself to be a better rider to get to the point that I felt that I was in control of the horse, or my body, enough to feel safe.

I eventually fell in love with equine rescue work which provided me an outlet to help the horses that had given me so much in my life. Let's be honest, it also allowed me to stay out of my own pain and issues. I could "fix" them instead of myself. My drive to run a rescue led me to a Bachelor of Science degree in equine studies, multiple certifications in equine massage therapy, and certifications in saddle fitting and flocking. I chased the ideal of being able to help horses while making plenty of cash per hour.

I started a business, I worked on a horse ambulance, and I worked for rescue organizations. I taught lessons to the next generation of horse lovers even though I didn't enjoy working with 5-12 year olds. It was a nice story but I didn't believe in my ability and I wasn't following my heart. Eventually I had a lot of knowledge and experience mixed with a heavy dose of burn out, loneliness, fear, and discontent.

So I stepped out of the horse world for a couple of years in pursuit of a desk job with a proper salary, paid vacation, and a retirement plan. I thought that if rescuing horses wasn't in the cards for me then I could make a bunch of money to ride for fun and donate to causes I cared about. Not surprisingly, after a few months I felt even more disconnected and yearned for passion and purpose in my life.

What was my solution? Yet another certification – this one as a holistic health coach. I was collecting bits of paper to prove that I was certifiably worthy to be me. I was saying to myself that it was going to be okay because *this* was surely the certification that would give me confidence or be the key to make a living doing something I love. Of course, I was wrong because I was chasing ideals rather than believing in myself.

The next set of certifications came a little closer to being aligned with my heart. I thought I had it figured out when I went and collected not one, but two, certifications as an equine specialist in equine assisted psychotherapy and learning. Now I *must* have my life purpose! I was close but I was still trying to walk someone else's path.

I tried the great rider and competitor path, the run a non-profit organization path, the work at a respectable job path, and the work within the mental health field path. The problem is that none of those were mine – I was trying to walk in other's shoes. I was carrying other's beliefs about money and business. I was carrying other's baggage about what life is supposed to look like.

More importantly, my heart was still broken from when I was a child. I was holding back my truth and authenticity. I was afraid to live my own life and allow my voice to be heard. I was full of self-doubt, limiting beliefs, anger, and sadness.

So I turned back to the horses who I knew would make my heart sing. I realized that I had to heal myself, learn to love myself, honor my strengths *and* vulnerabilities, and embrace my own uniqueness. I had to learn to accept all of my emotions to incorporate them into my life so that I could learn their lessons. I had to step into my own power to make my own music.

I also turned to spirituality in search of answers. I wanted to get to know myself. I wanted to fall in love with all of the things I labeled as good *and* bad that make up my inner landscape. I finally allowed myself to work with horses the way I wanted to rather than following the latest trends. I began to heal and listen to my heart and intuition through awareness and meditation. I fell in love with me and everything that I have to offer you.

I can't wait to meet you and hear your inspiring story. I can't wait to fall in love, alongside you and the horses, with all of your good and bad parts that make up your inner landscape. I can't wait to see you fall in love with yourself when you see your soul through the horse's eyes for the first time. I can't wait to embrace your heart on your journey to empowerment, self-love, and integrity. I can't wait for you to find the song of your soul and start dancing to that rhythm through life.

The questions is: How long are *you* willing to wait?

Chapter One:
Empowered Partnership

__Empowered:__ to give authority or power to
__Partnership:__ a relationship involving close cooperation between parties with joint rights and responsibilities

How glorious would it be if the result of training and riding horses was empowerment and emotional freedom for the horse and human alike? I believe it is time to take our work with horses to the next level and make that our new reality. While we used to rely on the horse for our basic needs, our relationship has shifted over the years and can now be one of self-actualization. So many riders want more from their relationship with their horse or feel that something is missing. These feelings stem from a mechanized way of interacting with horses. If we can learn how to step out of our limiting beliefs around training and shift into new creative methods of building partnerships, we will enrich the lives of our horses and discover a new way to live.

What would your life feel like if you were truly in love with yourself and felt worthy of greatness? I believe that each person is born into this world with a unique set of talents and challenges that can manifest into their highest purpose for walking this earth. We are so busy looking for the source of happiness *outside ourselves* that we miss out on the essence of beauty in each moment. Over time it feels as though our lives have slipped through our fingers and we are simply surviving rather than realizing our dreams. If we can learn to dive into our emotions and allow our hearts to start leading us through life, it will transform our experience. We can learn to thrive and celebrate life.

Wouldn't it feel wonderful if your horses were happy and eager to work with you every day and performed to the best of their ability? I believe that it is our responsibility to be of service to the animals in our care. Our interactions with horses are initiated by us – horses wouldn't choose of their own volition to interact with people in an intimate manner. Their lives are in our hands and we make the choices that determine the outcome of their experience in this world. We can change our approach to honor horses' wisdom and innate gifts so that they too can live with a deeper sense of peace and well-being. If we can encourage our horses to live up to their full potential they will be more content and we will achieve greater results in our training. Riding can then become a joyful dance between horses and humans.

What would the world be like if we raised our consciousness and lived in unity? I believe that we are all interconnected and each individual's actions have an impact on the energetic fabric of the universe. We all benefit when a person finds their passion and releases their beautiful contributions into the world. Every time a living being shifts into a more positive life the universe affirms and supports that shift. If we change our approach in the barn we can create ripples of energy that will positively impact our own lives, our horses' lives, and the lives of everyone. We have the power to make the world a better place and that can begin in a paddock.

The vision

My vision for Soulful Horsemanship is to utilize in the barn the wisdom of learning, questioning, and spirituality. We know that horses have the power to heal. We have seen them affect deep transformations on physical, mental, and emotional levels through therapeutic riding and equine assisted psychotherapy. That transformative power is available to every person who works with horses. When we combine the innate talents of horses with the spiritual concepts of humans, such as meditation, we can transcend our current limits. We can build partnerships that change the lives of horses and humans. We can each learn to live our best life and, as a result, change the world.

Soulful Horsemanship is about co-creation. It is more than just collaborating or working together with your horse on a task. Through co-creation both parties must be open to learning from the other to create something that is greater than either could have created or imagined on their own. In this model neither human nor horse imposes their opinions on the other but instead work together to mold their joint creation into something that both agree is beautiful and beneficial. It requires compromise throughout the process but the end result is uncompromising. The solution serves both parties and leads to bliss, empowerment, and a realization of our dreams. The horse and human learn to believe in and value themselves and each other and seek to serve one another's needs. We become both the teacher and the student.

The process to attain this is a reciprocal, dynamic, circular, and multifaceted interaction. The humans, as the ones who initiate the relationship, must be the first who are willing to give. In giving we receive wisdom and the horse receives an opportunity to grow. With that growth the horse has more to give which enables us to continue learning. There are no exact answers in this process but it is time for riders and horse owners to think independently and question the norms. It takes patience and understanding to form a partnership. We are so focused on what we want that we forget we are only half of the equation. There is a need to better understand the way of the horse and his true power. A need to be more empathetic, compassionate, and look at the way the horse experiences the world.

This new approach would not mean forsaking the knowledge that we have gained through the development of horsemanship. Nor does it mean that you must give up on your goals as an equestrian. Soulful Horsemanship is about embracing all of the knowledge and skill based information that is out there and filtering it through a new mental framework. We have explored the breadth of the horse/human relationship and now we have the opportunity to delve into the depth of it. We can move from the superficial motions of riding to an inspirational, meaningful relationship with the horse. There is the potential to dramatically change our riding and our lives if we change our perception and intention.

To initiate a change we need to take the next step in our evolution of interacting with horses. The equine industry made a huge leap forward over recent decades by choosing to work with horses in a new way. Leaders began to emerge in the industry who spoke out against the old methods of harshly breaking horses through pain and fear. The natural horsemanship industry emerged with a proliferation of new thought processes to promote a kinder, gentler way of training horses. I believe it is time to build on that and I hope to see an expansion of Soulful Horsemanship methods emerging in the industry. I think of traditional methods as a way to train through physical means, natural methods as a way to train through mental processes, and soulful methods as a way to connect from the heart.

The shift from body to mind to soul in horsemanship is reflective of the same shift that we are making in society as a whole. We are moving from external power and competition to internal power and cooperation. We are moving from masculine energy to feminine energy. We have physically conquered and controlled our environment and the horse. We then moved to a space of intellect and mental dominance over others. We now have the opportunity to approach everything, including the horse, in a new way. We can create a heart connection that honors others by being true to ourselves. We can benefit the whole by living in peace and harmony with the intention for our actions to be beneficial for everyone.

Soulful Horsemanship is about focusing more on your way of being and your emotional center so that you can be present with the horse, build a relationship, work in harmony, and ultimately gain better results in training. It's not only about teaching skills for the technical development of the horse and rider but also about teaching skills to develop awareness for the emotional development of both. Horses have the physical prowess to inspire people to express themselves. Humans have mental prowess to inspire horses to develop creatively. Where these gifts overlap is in the heart. Heart energy can be shared to build a web of connectivity. We can learn to interact from the divine power within each of us, where horse and human are one and equal, while utilizing the physical and mental strengths of each to enhance our training. It is so amazing to be in a supportive relationship that holds the space, or creates an energetic web of support, for both parties to embody their highest potential.

We cannot really have reverence for the horse until we learn to have reverence for ourselves. We must see our own unique beauty and talents to unlock our self-love and authentic power. With that inner wisdom we can shine our light out onto everyone we meet without ever dimming our own light. Giving to others, including the horse, takes nothing from us. A flame is not diminished by lighting another candle; the world just gets a little brighter. We can practice this with the horse. We can only gain by surrendering some of our control and righteousness over the horse. Through the process of healing the horse we restore their ability to help us heal. If we act in service to the horse, the horse will in turn seek to serve us, and we can find balance that makes the relationship greater than the sum of its parts.

With this philosophy the goal shifts from training riders and horses to improving the lives of both parties, where our interactions are the path to personal development, enrichment, and empowerment. Training becomes a means to address the emotional worlds, dreams, and desires of the horse and human. It is soul-centered horsemanship that brings a connection to spirit and one another in order to expand into a space grander than competent riders and well-behaved horses. We can utilize body awareness and mindfulness techniques to build a base that allows us to explore our emotional worlds and bring the gifts of the horse and individual into the world. While the intent of Soulful Horsemanship is personal growth and empowerment for horse and human alike, our actual training will also benefit and we will be able to take our horses farther in our chosen disciplines.

The focus of Soulful Horsemanship is to collaborate and help one another transform. We can change our motivation in training to identify how we can help the horse develop and how the horse can help us grow. Both parties can support and benefit one another. This is a shift from the one-sided approach of getting the horse to do what we want for our entertainment. We must overcome our need to dominate and control the horse so that we can find deeper connection and meaning with not only the horse but also ourselves, our communities, and our world. We have to approach our lives and our work with the horse from our heart rather than our head. The best things in life come from our heart and soul's connection and desire, not from our ego. A focus on the heart and soul will lead to the horse and human having a positive effect on one another and will leave us with a sense of belonging rather than just longing.

Growth opportunities for humanity

We all deserve to be healthy, happy, and fulfilled, and to realize our dreams. We are all here to play our part and bring our gifts into the world for the benefit of everyone. However, you can't find joy and peace or contribute your talents to the world if you do not know who you are and what gifts you have to give. We are so focused on our outer expression, looks, success, personas, and labels that we ignore our inner wisdom and truth. Until we learn to look within for guidance and to understand who we are, we will always feel pressure to find something more. Each of us has the power to change our lives and the lives of those around us but it takes great courage to do the personal work and make the necessary leap of faith. Horses can help guide us along the path to inner wisdom, emotional awareness, and purposeful living. But before we can look at ways to make changes, we have to examine who we are, our current way of life, and how we got here.

If we look at ourselves and the horse through compassionate eyes we can see that both are needlessly suffering to some degree. This awareness can lead us to change our approach to one of understanding and cooperation. We can team up with the horse to rise above the mundane. We can extend our heart to the horse and develop a deep desire to work in right relationship with them. If we choose a new path that comes from love and we are willing to let go of our prior training, conceptions, demands, and beliefs we can transcend our current state of being, both as a team and as an individual.

The process begins unfolding when you take a close look at your inner self, what you want, what you dream about, and what you identify as your deepest desires. In addition, you must see what is holding you back and the ways in which you feel disempowered. Most of us do not realize our full potential and limit ourselves through our belief systems, fear, doubt, and misunderstandings. Is your body healthy and balanced or do you have little respect and reverence for the temple in which you reside? Are you in control of your life or have your thoughts and emotions taken command? Are you living your life with purpose and meaning or are you living superficially, yearning for more?

We have followed the beliefs that were taught to us and those that we invented about ourselves. However, we, collectively, have the ability to help raise the consciousness of humanity to help heal the world. It is time to move to a connected state through love, compassion, forgiveness, joy, and peace. The way to change yourself is by changing your beliefs. Do not separate yourself from others and the universe. You are one with everything

We have made agreements with ourselves and society that keep us bound, rather than allowing us to do what feels good. Often we feel powerless in our lives. We feel as though life is happening to us and we have no control. We are out of touch with our emotional worlds. Things happen in our lives that we don't understand or have a hard time accepting.

Most people walk around living a life that is a fraction of who they have the potential to become. We are much more powerful than we realize. It is easy to shy away from that power because, with an acknowledgement of how much we control our lives, we must also take responsibility. If our self-worth is based on external circumstances, we can blame those things instead of looking within to change our ways. Breaking patterns and beliefs is difficult and it can be painful to let go of the self-created image. Whether we choose to accept it or not, we have untapped potential if we are willing to challenge those old patterns and beliefs.

We tend to live an ego-based life, rather than a soul-based life. The ego creates a false perception of separation. People are starving for deeper connection, purpose, and meaning. We have lost the connections with ourselves, our communities, and our families. Our society has created an ethos that success is achieved by the individual and it is this emphasis on the individual that prevents us from working together. As long as we view ourselves as separate there is a need to prove ourselves, to be right, to be liked, and to be accepted by the group - but that prevents us from stepping into the full potential of our lives. If we see ourselves as interconnected and part of everyone else then we can shift to a soul-based life that serves our greater purpose and meets our true desires in life.

Our society has suppressed our intuition by ruling through dominance, fear, intimidation, and obedience. It is time for us to awaken our spirits and discover our true essence. We are taught to focus on making money, becoming famous, and winning, all of which are ways to exert external power. However, when the outcome is more important than the activity we stop living and start striving. If we can shift to authentic power we will find peace and understanding. With authentic power we no longer need to separate ourselves and make ourselves distinguished because we have self-worth and self-love. It is then possible to see that we are all interconnected and we are all worthy. We can come to recognize that helping others succeed helps us to succeed.

We try to separate and prove ourselves by being better, thinner, faster, smarter, worthier, and more important. We worry that if we let go of our labels about who and what we are then we will lose our identity. Deep down we know that our external persona is not who we truly are and so we use it as a shield to protect ourselves. However, as long as we hide behind masks we will never live the life that we are destined to live. It can be scary to step out of our ruts for fear that others will judge us, but the truth is that others will follow because everyone is ultimately searching for the same things in life. If you find the courage to follow your heart, you can become an inspiration for others in your life to awaken.

How do we relate to horses?

The societal beliefs and values in which we are steeped also affect the way that we keep and work with horses. We have passed down the traditions and techniques of horsemanship from a time in which we had to command obedience from horses for our very survival. We continue to perpetuate a dominance-submission paradigm and training model that no longer serves our needs. We must look at our interactions with horses in an honest and defenseless manner in order to decide for ourselves if we want to continue managing and training horses according the status quo or if we are ready to revolutionize our approach.

It is easy to approach animals with a sense of entitlement. We are human and they are beast. However, if we begin to see everything as interconnected and of the same spirit then we can bridge the gaps to find our similarities rather than focusing on our differences. As we seek a partnership with the horse, we cannot view ourselves as superior. Entitlement leads us to believe that we have the right to get what we want regardless of the horse's needs and wants. Our horse's opinions, activities, and insights are not beneath us, they are just different and a gift from which we can learn. Is it really okay to impose our will on anyone else? That is the work of ego, not spirit. Furthermore, the horse does not look at us as superior. He may look at us as a predator but he does not instinctually know that humans are considered to be "top dog" and better than all the rest. That label is, after all, a product of the human ego. The horse does not automatically understand or respect our talents and intellect.

The horse's true essence revolves around freedom of movement – this is where their power originates. The horse's language, survival, intuition, joy, playfulness, safety, and experience come through his body. It is through this magnificent expression of form that humans are able to rejoice in the equine experience. Whether it is watching a stallion run in open space, witnessing a foal stagger on her gangly legs in the first moments of life, or being carried on the back of your favorite gelding, we are in awe of the horse's power and grace.

However, humans restrict the horse's movement in every possible way and in doing so disempower him. We strip from him the very qualities that make us admire him. We need to understand the ways in which we make the horse less confident, deprive him of power, authority and influence, and how we make him weak, ineffectual, and unimportant. We need to look at the ways that we control the horse through fear, pain, manipulations, and demands in order to find a way to return his autonomy.

Humans control every aspect of the horse – his external and internal movement, self-expression, and social scenarios. We decide if a horse gets turned out, for how long, and with whom. We decide when, what, and how much the horse eats. We decide who works with, owns, and rides him. We decide the type, length, and intensity of his work. We do all of this in the name of management and training but none of it gives the horse a say or makes sense to the horse. It is all designed around our benefit, enjoyment, and ease.

When we work with the horse it is a series of demands. On the ground we drive him away from us in all directions in the hope of developing closeness and connection. Does that even make sense? The horse must always yield to pressure or suffer the consequence. We shout at him with our body. On his back we "school" him – move forward, not like that, put a foot here, get off my hand, a little faster now, turn, lift, look this way. And on it goes for an hour. He is asked to move fluidly and willingly under a saddle that often restricts movement or causes pain. The horse is unable to comprehend a reason for all of this. He tries to express himself only to be punished as we strip away his personality and treat him as a machine or a toy. There is no balance of power in this type of relationship.

We give the horse little choice in any of our interactions with him. For example, if a horse goes to grab a bite of food while on trail, which is what he is hardwired to do, we simultaneously pull on his mouth and kick him in the ribs. He is punished for foraging, which is how he survives, because we want a nice ride and require that he submit to our desire over his own. In addition, our actions are based on outdated purpose. For example, all riders are taught to always mount on the left side of their horse. This does not create a well-balanced horse and is completely unnecessary. It had a purpose in the Calvary so that right handed soldiers would not have to swing their sword over when they mounted but, unless you ride with a sword on your left hip, it is unnecessary.

Some horses do genuinely love their job. Some are lucky enough to enjoy the work they have been chosen to do. There is no doubt that there are horses who love to work cattle, jump, or gallop with a herd out foxhunting. They enjoy having an outlet to use their mind and body. Horses love to play. On the flip side they are wired to not over exert themselves and they do not necessarily see any intrinsic value in carrying humans in circles. They also need a reason behind their work to stay fresh and interested. Each is an individual with different needs, wants, and likes and we should honor that to ensure that they are willing participants in our fun and games. The process that we go through to get the horse proficient enough to perform his job, even if it is a job he ultimately enjoys, needs to be looked at differently.

We must examine our motivations for owning and riding horses. Is it completely selfish? What is the purpose, not just for us, but also the horse? Are we unintentionally enslaving the horse and managing him in a tyrannical fashion or are we actively seeking ways to liberate the horse by encouraging him with patience and generosity? We have been asking the horse to work a minimum wage job with no benefits. In our society we place great emphasis on careers and know that we must work to earn a paycheck to meet our needs. This is not the horse's reality. All the horse has to do is put his head down to eat and make sure he flees from predators. We ask the horse to exert his precious energy to carry us and perform and assume that the care we give him is a good enough paycheck. The horse is incapable of that type of reasoning.

We must also examine our reasons for riding. What do we really get out of it? Is it only about competition and winning blue ribbons? Is it really to have an all-terrain vehicle to take us out cross country? Of course not. There is something about the horse that gets under our skin. Some of us get a taste for it and can't let it go. Some of us spend our entire lives daydreaming about horses. Those of us who ride do so because we love horses, particularly that one special horse that we call our own. We feel drawn to them in a way that can't be shaken – not by time constraints, financial worries, or broken bones. Some of us feel incomplete without a horse in our lives. Rather than focusing on all the outer results of riding, why not focus on the inner transformation that comes from working with horses? Why not delve into their magnificence that fills us with an unshakable desire to be part of their world?

Can we begin to question our methods and attitudes? Horses live in captivity. That is a fact that we cannot change. Nor should we want to. Horses and humans have come together in a fantastic manner throughout history and that should not be lost. It would be a disservice to the horse and human to no longer work together.

However, it is our responsibility to understand the way of the horse and how he experiences the world. It is necessary to take a close look at how the horse's natural instincts are affected by living in a human world. He has lost his freedom and relies on humans, deadly predators, to care for him. It is time to shift from ego-driven, self-centered demands of the horse to an empathetic, compassionate partnership with the horse.

Horses rely on humans to care for them but that doesn't mean that they should feel trapped, scared, shut down, diminished, or in need of defending themselves. We have the ability to help the horse to feel spontaneous joy, freedom, and power. We would be well rewarded to allow them to live an empowered life and to live their truth. We are so focused on teaching horses the way of the human that we have forgotten to allow them to teach us the way of the horse. If we open up to their vibration, wisdom, power, and freedom of spirit we could learn a lot. If we see them for who they really are we can honor them rather than coerce them to perform for us and behave within our limitations.

Humans and horses are living within the constraints of the human world, society, and old belief systems. We dull the horse by imposing our societal beliefs onto him and try to make him fit into our human world but we do the same thing to ourselves – to our soul. Just as we have restricted the horse, we have confined ourselves within the boundaries of a mediocre life. Both horse and human are wishing for a different outcome, wanting more from life, and hoping to be understood. We have the power to change the current paradigm of viewing ourselves as unworthy passengers through life and working with the horse as beast of burden. We can team up with horses to initiate positive change.

A shift in partnership

Horsemanship has only focused on the results, skills, and techniques to care for, train, and ride horses. It has been a successful system developed through centuries to manage horses and produce riders. However, somewhere in the process we forgot that we are teaching humans – complex people with hopes and fears – to train horses – sentient beings with desires and aversions. We have ignored the heart and soul of the work in favor of systems and outcomes. We forgot about the inner worlds of the horse and the human.

We have approached horses as a way to exert our desires, fulfill our needs, and gain benefit and pleasure. While this can be enjoyable and make us feel better it is not a lasting feeling of joy and it isn't beneficial to the horse. There can be a different way – a way to help the horse and make lasting internal change. In modern times we ride for the joy of it. Because riding is no longer a necessity, we can approach the horse with love and compassion. We can develop a better partnership with our horses, be more successful in training, help our horses to live richer lives, and learn awareness of our thoughts and feelings to allow our authentic power to unfold.

A lot of people are looking for deeper connection in our disjointed world so those of us who dream of horses turn to them in hopes of becoming part of their herd. We seek out a relationship with the horse to fill a void in our lives. Unfortunately, in a desperate attempt to make our horse a friend and someone that we can bond with we often approach the relationship in an unhealthy manner. Some of us coddle and baby the horse with no clear respect for the necessary boundaries of a relationship with a 1,200 pound animal. Though the horse can be a friend and confidant who provides solace and healing, we must honor him for who he is and not who we would like him to be. The other end of the spectrum is the individuals who try to force compliance in the relationship by controlling the horse and making him conform to the rules of relationship as defined by the human.

In trying to be nice so that the horse will like us, we lose respect for ourselves. In attempting to force a relationship onto the horse, we lose respect for the horse. Partnership cannot be attained in this manner because there isn't balance. This type of dynamic requires one member of the team to be devalued for the benefit of the other. We can't allow the horse to walk all over us nor should we attempt to push him around. When we try so hard to create a positive relationship we actually prevent it from taking shape. An honest look at the current dynamic with our horses is our first opportunity for growth and learning.

If we look at our relationship with our horses we may see the same dynamics playing out in other important relationships in our lives. For example, do I belittle my value or lose my individuality to appease others? Or am I more inclined to overpower, control, or manipulate others to get what I want? Do I view myself as less or greater than others? Do I contribute in a positive, negative, or neutral way in my relationships? Do I respect others for who they are? By examining the ways that we try to establish a working relationship with the horse we gain insights into our belief system about ourselves and relationships. Are our attempts to build a partnership working? Why or why not? What changes can we make to have more authentic interactions?

We must ask ourselves how controlling the horse makes us feel. Is it a healthy form of power? How do these feelings play out in our life and our inner self? Unfortunately, many of us resort to grasping for external power because we do not know what it means to live with inner power – authentic power. So we do the only thing we know how to do which is to dominate the horse and create rules that we enforce with dictator-like methods. We are exacting to a fault in our training at the expense of the horse. This is not necessarily our intention. We are looking for empowerment but don't know how to find it so we turn to the horse, the symbol of power and freedom, to find a way rise above everything. There is nothing like time in the barn or on the back of a horse to make the world look like a better place.

In a way this control, dominance, and external power over an animal so much bigger and stronger than us is empowering. We feel good about ourselves for achieving results and getting the horse to perform for us. We feel free for those moments that we are astride such a magnificent animal. We are able to achieve many things in this manner but this doesn't build our authentic power or lasting freedom and, instead, serves to diminish the power and freedom of the horse. As long as we feed into the old paradigms of dominance and submission we will not find lasting change for either party. We need to shift the power dynamics from an external process to an internal process and give the horse back his authenticity. We do not need to take his power – we can become empowered by empowering him. When we do, riding can be built on trust, understanding, and communication.

We can combine our desires with the needs of the horse in a holistic, compassionate manner. To do that we must let go of our agendas and selfish manner. It is possible to raise each other up in a symbiotic, collaborative way that is mutually beneficial. We can train the horse with love, empathy, compassion, and passion and, in the process, find ourselves. Coming together can be a journey of self-discovery, self-expression, and spiritual awakening, all of which are keys to unlocking self-love, authentic power, and our purpose in life. With intuition and intention we can have a positive impact on the horse while gaining insights about ourselves. We can still master the art of riding while simultaneously improving our lives. We can create something beautiful.

We can meet our needs in a more holistic manner that also takes the horse's needs into consideration by forming a partnership. A partner is defined as one that takes part in an undertaking with another with shared risks and profit. A partner is one that is united with another in an activity or sphere of common interest. If we approach our horse with the idea that we are partners then we must be willing to take equal risks and ensure that both are gaining an equal profit from our work together. We must also ensure that our work together, whatever the activity, is of interest to both. A partnership should be entered into freely. This is a very different perspective than our current way of thinking. Most equestrians have a preferred discipline, purchase a horse that has the athletic ability to perform, trains him to have the skills to be successful in the activity that we chose, and insist that he do his job or face the consequences of being punished or sold.

The end product of training is a seasoned horse that can carry us on a trail ride, perform the moves in a dressage test, or pull a carriage. Those skills should be the joyous expression of the development of a partnership rather than an outlet to let off steam after being dominated for years. What matters is all of the steps to get us to that end expression and the reason behind the work. The end result can be sweeter for both horse and rider if the journey there is savored. Both need to feel a regular sense of accomplishment through meaningful work. The horse must understand the process and have an opinion. In this new type of training we will ask our horse to do the same type of self-development work that we are undertaking. We are going to support one another on a journey of self-discovery and self-actualization.

So the next step in our evolution with the horse is synergistic partnership in which we come together to help one another and to create something greater than either could have on their own. We can develop an environment that enables, supports, and empowers the team. With this perspective it is important to understand that both the human and the horse must give to the process and get something valuable out of the process or it is not equal and worth it to everyone involved. In this type of relationship we cannot view one party as better or worse – we must see ourselves as interconnected equals.

A new way to interact

How do we join forces with the horse to go about helping one another? Let's face it, horses and humans are not the most likely partners. We have different goals in life, social structures, abilities, physical make up, and language. One is a prey animal and the other a predator. There is a fair amount to overcome to become equal partners but each has something that can help the other to grow and develop. We can learn to read one another and communicate authentically to travel side by side down a path to joy, love, and peace. In learning to overcome the obstacles to equal partnership with the horse, we can learn to relate to everyone and everything in a new manner. We can begin to see the value and innate beauty in all things. We can begin to see the complexities of interactions between beings and the simplicity of the essence within each of us.

Working with the horse gives us an opportunity to practice taking risks on our path to a bigger life. If we have a genuine desire to improve our lives and build a strong relationship with the horse we can work through the discomfort required to get to a place that is so much more fulfilling and meaningful. Just as a soul-based, passionate life eventually leads us to asking how we can serve others, we must shift our perspective to how we can help and serve the horse. The horse is also driven by the desire for pleasure and the avoidance of pain. It is possible to stop motivating him to work *for* us through fear-based training and the avoidance of pain and inspire him to work *with* us through love-based training and the desire for pleasure.

If we are successful in allowing the horse to be true to himself while working in partnership with us then he can become a sounding board for our questions about our journey and who we are. Making a choice to do this is part of the growth process. Giving the horse a choice helps him but it also gives us a chance to work on ourselves. Are we attached to thoughts, ideas, or behavior patterns? What stories do we tell ourselves about who we are in relation to the horse? Would part of our identity shatter if we approached the horse in a different manner? Would it harm our ego to listen to the horse? How would it make our heart feel? Would allowing the horse to choose something different threaten us? The process starts with us. We gain a benefit by releasing control. In turn the horse steps into his power and the empowered horse can help us further. This is the symbiosis.

We can begin returning some of their power and freedom, not by turning them loose or not working with them, but by playing with them and working in a joyful manner. There will always be things that we do with horses that they don't particularly like or understand, such as having their teeth floated, but that does not mean that we give up and make no effort to change our perspective to provide the horse some autonomy. Even if your goal is to compete you will get so much more out of it if your horse performs with confidence, pride, and inspiration. Recognizing the pitfalls in the horse/human relationship does not mean that you have to stop riding, get rid of all of your equipment, or berate yourself. It is simply an opportunity to look through compassionate eyes and, if it feels right to you, make a change in your approach and intent. You can have a positive effect on your horse and in return reap the benefits of his wisdom.

Horses should have a choice in their participation, movement, and expression. They have feelings and should be free to live authentically as they are – they are an equine and an individual with their own personality. They should have the ability to agree or disagree, to walk away, or to change the direction of a training session. While it is good to have a horse that will listen to us, we must let go of the demand for him to cooperate and do what we want. Our riding and training would be much improved if we had a horse that wants to listen to us but who is also heard. We are the ones that desire a partnership with the horse and we need to show him that it can be beneficial to him to team up with us.

Horses need to see that we have insights that can make them feel good and have a positive impact on their lives. Rather than focusing on how we can get the horse to perform specific movements we can change our perspective to how we can make suggestions to help him improve his movement. We can look at it as a way to help him with his quality and type of movement as a form of self-exploration that is beneficial to him. As a being that uses his body to sense and communicate information, the horse can benefit from learning body awareness and how to move and express himself in new ways.

Soulful Horsemanship does not mean that we let the horse have all the say and control in the relationship. Rather we take a step back to raise the horse up to the level of an equal. It is not fair for either party to always get their way. Both must be heard, understood, and valued for the part they play. We can learn to listen and trust that the horse may have a better idea and work in collaboration with him rather than assuming that we are always right. We can complement one another and find compromise for the needs of everyone to be met. Both the human and the horse can learn when to listen and give in versus when to stand up for themselves and say no. The creation of healthy boundaries is integral to teamwork.

Allowing horses to act authentically with us enables us to unlock the potential for them to help us on our path. Horses live in the present moment and are masters at reading energy. This ability means they are able to continually sense an individual's inner state of being and will react accordingly. We create and project personas and stories that are not always authentic to our actual mental-emotional state. Without the ability to understand words, the horse never becomes confused by these projections. We cannot fool a horse or win him over with outward gestures – he reads who we are through the energy that we emanate and, therefore, has a window into our inner world. Watching how a horse reacts to an individual gives insight that can help that individual make changes to improve her life. This innate ability in the horse is a gift. If we are open to it, horses can teach us about ourselves, how to live in the present, and how to better read energy.

The horse can act as a mirror but the image that they reflect is not the outer shell that we normally see – he shows our emotions and core belief systems. This is best demonstrated when working with horses at liberty when they are free to be expressive. We all carry baggage from the past and have insecurities about the future which can lead us to living a life full of anger, resentment, jealousy, fear, sadness, or inadequacy. We need to understand the things that are holding us back from living our best life. We also need to see how our emotions are projected onto others, even when we try to mask them. Horses can help illuminate those dark spaces so that the individual can begin to address them.

When we are working with horses that are empowered, they will react to what we actually believe rather than what we say we believe. Some of us act confident and capable when in reality we don't believe in ourselves or our ability. Maybe we manage to fool everyone in our life. Maybe we over compensate by bullying coworkers or bragging about our accomplishments. The horse will be able to see through all of that. If we ask a horse to do something without believing in ourselves the horse isn't going to trust us. If we fall back on our "tough guy" tactics to prove ourselves the horse will balk and move away because we aren't acting authentically. This allows us to peel back the layers and see the core of the matter which then allows us to make changes. When we have successfully shifted and start to believe in ourselves, the horse will trust us and work in partnership, giving us immediate, positive feedback. Regardless of our issues, awareness is the catalyst for personal growth and empowerment.

Horses already see us for who we are and can reflect our thought processes and feelings for us to examine. They can help us see our negative thinking, where we are stuck, and what we really want out of life. If we give them the chance they can help us unlock our spiritual warrior and get in touch with who we really are. You are not just a body going through the motions but a soul here to grow, create, and express. Interacting with horses in an authentic way can help us to uncover our strengths and weakness, discover our passion, and live a full, happy life.

Horses can show us how to listen to universal wisdom without the ego so that we can live out the true desires of our heart and soul. They can help us embrace spirit through self-awareness. They can provide us with a sounding board to work through the areas in which we are struggling. As we take steps to restore balance in the horse's life we are also going to come up against self-doubt, programmed thinking, and repetitive behavior. Facing these challenges will shake out our belief system and present opportunities to work through areas in our life that could use a little attention. If we really want to improve our lives the horse will help, but in return he deserves our help.

Making the choice to change

Ultimately it is our choice if we even want to go down this path. Illuminating our emotions can be scary and hard work. Some of us may feel it is easier to stay in the dark and continue doing what we know because it feels safe. But I believe we deserve more. We deserve to live a peaceful life full of love and happiness – and so do our horses. We have brought horses into our lives for a reason. Perhaps it is simply because we love them or maybe because, on a soul level, we know that they can help us to heal.

Evolution is a long process and change doesn't happen overnight. We are on a journey through life in search of ways to improve the manner in which we think, move, feel, experience, express, and live. However, we have been practicing the patterns of our lives for years and it will take time to approach both life and our interactions with the horse in a new way. It will also take the horse awhile to unlearn old behaviors and defense mechanisms so we must be patient, understanding, and compassionate. Partnership takes effort and doesn't come easily or just by thinking about it. This journey is about the effort, not the goal. When we want to arrive at our goals more than we want to be doing what we are doing we become stressed. Anything providing a lot of joy and freedom is worth the risk.

Soulful Horsemanship is about finding our own truth, serving others, and feeling good rather than trying to prove ourselves. Others' views and opinions should not affect our choices or we stop living authentically and start changing who we are to please them. By nature we need to feel safe and valued but to get to that point we often look for outside validation or something external to make us whole. External things, others' opinions, and material possessions cannot create an inner state. Only we can create the value, safety, and confidence that will allow us to chip away at the negative thoughts, feel all of our emotions, and open up to a world of self-love, joy, and inner peace. We must do our work to rise above the ego and find our connection to everything.

With choice comes the power to see that we are creators in our lives and have the responsibility to really live rather than just react to circumstances. We have the opportunity to break out of the ruts that we have been taught to follow and instead follow our heart. When we look outside ourselves hoping someone else will give us the answers or tell us what to do, we stop being true to ourselves and start living someone else's life. This leaves us powerless and unhappy. To awaken we must first accept that we have been asleep. We have not been "wrong" in our approach to life, or horses, but we have shut off our connection to our internal self in preference for "easy" conditioned responses that felt safe and familiar. We do not have a signed contract to continue living that way.

Situations will arise to allow us to choose self-worth and love over doubt and fear. The same is true with the horse. We give him opportunities to learn but he must choose to change – that is his work. We can't own anyone else's struggle, work, or path. We cannot change others but we can change ourselves from the inside out. If we find the courage to look within and make a different decision it will be reflected in our horses, our relationships, and our world. Each of us must take responsibility for the part that we play without resisting the bad or grasping for the good. The horse cannot make us whole – nothing and no one can do that except for ourselves – but he can help us see the truth about ourselves. The only things that we really have to believe in are ourselves and our horses and we must have a genuine desire to improve the lives of both.

We need to think outside the box to a space where conventional meets inspirational. We can use all of our knowledge and theory as a base and then surrender to the process and the unknown. We may not have all the answers initially but with the horse we can find our own truth. We can make soul goals rather than head goals. If we keep empowered partnership as the point to continually return to, we can learn to love ourselves and the horse for what we are rather than what we wish we were. We are not mediocre.

Find connection to the harmony of the universe through nature, spirituality, or the way of the horse. See the divinity in yourself and others. Spirit is within your horse and your heart speaking the truth through the vibrations of love. If we treat everyone as though they are part of the divine it would leave us in a state of awe and compassion. We wouldn't hurt people, wage war, or let others starve. We wouldn't view the horse as our servant or something we own. As a part of God we have an awesome responsibility to ourselves, everyone, and everything in the universe. Dream big and have goals but live and act now. You have divine wisdom now.

Don't choose to do something different in the future. Choose to do it now. Change happens here, in this moment, not out there or in the future. Life is full of pure, unlimited potential and we have the ability to embrace our wildest dreams and make them a reality. We can't just wish for fulfillment, emotional freedom, and partnership with the horse. We must be willing to change, challenge old belief systems, and become completely honest with ourselves. We must do the work.

You create your reality and you deserve to live up to your full potential. You only have one life to experience everything you want so don't hold yourself back. Believe in yourself. This is your life – right now. What do you want to do with it? Every day, every moment is a gift that you never get to repeat. Accept the challenge, take charge, change your perception, and change the world. Your choices determine how you spend your day and how you spend your days determines how you live your life. This is not a dress rehearsal. There are no second takes and there is not necessarily a chance to get it right later. This is it. Just as your horse deserves to be empowered, so do you. You are a piece of spirit, a sacred being that deserves to be loved and live the best life possible.

Divine energy continuously flows together and through one another. As you clean up your life you can help to clean up the world. By embracing your power you can help everyone live their highest purpose. We are one mind, one heart. The changes you put into effect have the power to change everyone. It does not detract from you when you help others to rise. We must work together and not try to outdo one another. Before awakening, we are stuck in the perception of separation. As we come to know our own truth, we become open to the perception of a unified consciousness. We can move from a state of emotional reaction to living in a more neutral state of awareness. We can begin to experience the beauty and joyfulness of our soul's personality rather than the ego's persona. We can embrace our oneness. Dream big, live big. The horse can help you if you let him.

Chapter Two:
Transformed Perspective

Transform: to change in structure, appearance or character
Perspective: a view of things in their true relationship or relative importance

This book is not designed as a "how-to manual" to teach you how to ride or train horses. If that is where you are on your path, there are hundreds of other books that can guide you and provide you with answers. This book is my overarching philosophy on teaching, training, and living, all of which is aligned with my spirituality. I believe that within each of us we have the wisdom and ability to answer questions, solve problems, and find solutions to change our relationships and ourselves.

My thoughts are designed to provide you with a compass that you can align with your heart to find your own way to your highest potential in and out of the arena. I believe that the horse amplifies the clarity of your destination by acting like the mirror on a sighting compass so that you can see exactly where you are headed in life. Through a vision that is aligned with your heart, your higher self, and your divinity you can build an amazing partnership with your horse and change your life.

This philosophy is something that can be sprinkled throughout your training process. If you are in the midst of preparing for a big event or competition season, there is no need to stop what you are doing. If you are learning to ride confidently on trails for fun, continue having fun. I encourage you to start filtering your experience through a transformed perspective to see how

Soulful Horsemanship can expand your depth of experience. Start by using the techniques in this book within your current framework. Follow your own truth to uncover what does and does not work for your unique partnership. Listen to your own wisdom to break free from your limitations. Allow a softening to unfold in you and slowly awaken to a new way of being.

In order to dive into the process of changing our perspective and developing an empowered partnership we must first look at the foundation for this methodology, the basic outline of concepts that will be covered throughout the remainder of this book, and some examples of how this process can manifest. I suggest you question everything you have ever been taught and everything that I say. At the center of this work are your heart, soul, and emotions. It is through embracing those things that you will find the stillness and awareness to listen to your own wisdom, your horse's insights, and your spiritual truth.

Creating a safe environment

Before you even begin your work with the horse, you have to start from a feeling of safety and security for both the horse and the human. All of the basic needs have to be met including proper diet, plenty of water, exercise, shelter, and rest. On top of that you both need to have your social needs met and feel as though you are part of family, community, and a herd. You have to both start from a place of health and well-being. Both must be safe, and *feel* safe, before bonding can begin. If either of you are focused on your base needs being met, it will leave you no energy or attention for growth and learning. Take an inventory of yourself and the horse and set your sights on a new way to do things. After your basic needs are met there is nothing holding you back from true happiness but your perspective and connection to the universe.

"Safety first" is a common thing to hear in barns and riding programs and I couldn't agree more. However, we must expand our understanding of that simple phrase because it is currently a reflection of physical safety for riders. If we maintain that point of view, without including physical safety for the horse, it can lead to dominant behavior to restrict the horse to ensure that he is safe to work around. We must view it as physical safety for people <u>and</u> horses. In this work we must also take it one step further to the idea of creating emotional safety for the human and horse.

Too often students are emotionally wrecked after a lesson. We are taught to check our feelings at the gate and to "get over it," which is precisely how we approach feelings in our society. We cannot find emotional awareness and empowerment if we are in an environment where we are expected to suppress our feelings. In addition, it is common for riding instructors to scream at and berate their students. This does not have a beneficial effect on anyone in the arena.

The horse is also asked to suppress his feelings when we work with him. Although it is important to create and maintain boundaries to ensure a safe physical space, the horse must be able to find his voice and be heard in this work. If he is heard and respected there will be less of a tendency for explosive outbursts in the future, reducing the need to control him. It is imperative to create a safe space for all parties to truly succeed. Soulful Horsemanship expands into learning about ourselves, communication, and relationships. We cannot develop awareness, compassion, intuition, and feeling if we are physically or emotionally unsafe or unbalanced.

Start by ensuring the barn and arena are a sacred place for people and horses. The barn is your horses' home so the first thing we need to do is clean up the way we manage them and the energy of the barn. We have a chance to change the way we do things by asking what barn management techniques would make the horses more secure and happy. We must ensure that their needs are met. The areas that horses are most commonly lacking are space, turn out, and company. Isolation is terrifying to horses so we should respect that and provide a stable herd for them to live in so that they feel comfortable and secure.

We should also ensure that their physical health needs are met, including their feet and teeth. For horses to want to work they have to be comfortable and sound. This gives us an opportunity to ensure that we are meeting their needs in a safe and respectful manner. Think about how scary the farrier or dentist is from your horses' perspective. We tend to punish them for not cooperating but we are asking them to allow a stranger to handle the most important parts of the horse – the feet and mouth. While these are necessary tasks it is up to us to teach them through compassion and patience how to handle that stimulus. It is not fair for the horse to be unprepared nor is it up to the professional to train the horse.

This is also a time to ensure that all of our equipment is in good working order, appropriate, and properly fitted. We should check our bits and determine if we want to make any changes. We should also check the fit of our saddle. We want to ensure that it is in good condition and that it still fits the horse. Often the horse has already been telling us there is an issue with the saddle by pinning his ears when we approach with it. In the past we may have ignored this behavior but moving forward it will be a cue to figure out if the saddle fits, if the horse is in pain, and if he has invited us into his space.

We also need to look at the feel of the overall environment at our barn, particularly at boarding facilities where we can't manage everything ourselves and there are other horses, riders, and trainers that may have an impact on our horses. The horse will be affected by everything and everyone that is in his living environment. If the person who used the indoor before us resorted to smacking her horse over a fence with a crop the energy in that space may feel different to your horse. If you are riding while someone else's trainer stands in the middle of the arena yelling at and belittling her student, your horse is going to pick up on it. Horses are so sensitive that they tune into their rider but also everyone else in the environment. We need to help them manage all of that feedback and ensure that we are in a space that is conducive to building a partnership based on empowerment, freedom, trust, and love.

Building your foundation

We are on a spiritual journey but we still need to have a solid base of knowledge about horses, riding, and training. Seeking help from a professional is essential to understanding how the horse moves and thinks so we can build body awareness and balance in ourselves and attain the necessary skills to be comfortable around the horse and on his back. It takes years to learn all of the basics and we never stop learning. For example, an independent seat is essential so that we can ride in balance without holding onto or relying on the horse to support us. An independent seat allows us to communicate effectively and build our confidence while preventing us from hindering the horse. We can practice the independent seat on our own but we need guidance and support to develop this cornerstone.

Working under the instruction of a skillful individual is imperative when you are learning to work with horses. Because there is so much to learn about horsemanship, beginners tend to latch onto their instructor. Unfortunately, it is easy to take that one person's methods as gospel truth. If you happen to learn things one way then you think that's the right way or the only way. Everyone benefits from studying with a wide range of people. You must also filter information and teaching through your own instinct and belief system. Don't give your trainer's advice so much weight that you lose your own voice. Be careful when choosing a trainer. Not only are you learning her methodology, but your horse is also going to pick up on her energy and authenticity. If she lacks confidence, is angry, or is impatient the horse will be affected.

With every horse trainer out there you can find a new approach and technique that is based on that individual's experience, teachers, and attitude. It's the attitude that you need to be careful about. There is a lot of ego in the horse world that can get in the way of discovering your own approach or encouraging you to build partnership with the horse. If a relationship with a particular trainer doesn't feel right, don't be afraid to say "no, thank you" regardless of how good or well-known they are. You are paying for that time to be about you and your growth. If the instructor makes you feel bad about yourself, asks you to do things you are not comfortable with, or treats the horse as a tool, then you have every right to look for someone else to work with. You do not have to take lessons from a bully.

Many instructors can teach you how to physically, or even mentally, respond to the horse and can teach you all of the basic objectives in riding. The greatest teachers connect on an emotional, spiritual, and soul level. In order to do that they must be present, aware, and hold the space for you. Some great riders find that the techniques that are so useful for them don't resonate with others. This is because they are not teaching the underlying intent, state of being, and feeling that goes along with the physical action. The underlying stuff, which is so hard to teach, holds all of the true power to inspire the horse to perform. So then the instructor may fall back on physically dominating methods to get the desired results and the entire experience suffers. Or, they yell at the student or blame the horse out of frustration. They have gotten caught up in technique and performance and lost the true power and connection.

You would not be very well educated if your first grade teacher was still your professor in college nor would you be very well-rounded if you took English to the exclusion of all other courses for your entire life. Be open to all different manners of riding and training. Hold onto the parts that resonate with you and apply those skills when the situation warrants it. No one person or book is going to teach you all you need to know. Most importantly, never forget that the best teacher you will ever meet is your horse.

Knowledge is power. Don't be afraid to think outside of your discipline. Learn from people in other specialties. They can shed new light on issues and inspire you to try new things if you are open and approach it with non-judgment. Growing up as a hunter/jumper rider, I turned my nose up at the entirety of western riding and missed out on an enormous wealth of knowledge and experience. Never stop learning. Don't get complacent and focus only on one methodology, trainer, guru, horse whisperer, or equine goddess. No single person has all the answers. No single method is right 100% of the time. Pull truth from as many people as you can and use it as inspiration to create your own masterpiece.

A lot of training and riding instruction involves giving the student a recipe to follow. There is little room for self-discovery and inspiration if you simply follow the moves and techniques taught by a specific instructor. The real magic happens when you incorporate various techniques and methodologies to create your own successful system. True riding is about your internal state, self-discovery, creativity, and joy. Learn from others – they can help you, and it would be foolish to waste their knowledge – but put it into your own framework for you and your horse.

Much of riding is about feel and that can't be taught. To develop that feel takes time with the horses, the right attitude, and awareness. Once you learn the basics, learn about safety, and develop your balance with the help of an instructor, riding becomes an art. Lessons are extremely important but you can't be fully aware and reacting to your horse in the moment when you are also trying to do what the instructor is telling you. Take your time to practice and follow your gut instincts. Patience and depth of understanding will carry you further in the long run. Develop your balance, understanding, and emotional awareness by working with a safe horse and compassionate trainer. From there you can start to ride out of the stillness.

How is Soulful Horsemanship different?

Soulful Horsemanship is about using your intuition and the guidance of spirit to help form a more meaningful relationship with the horse and yourself. Anyone can use it. Following specific training methods is the way of the mind. We want all the answers to be provided. That is how we are trained to learn and think. It is also easier and more comfortable to have someone else provide us with solutions. However, a training method that works for one person will not necessarily work for you. You have to filter others' methods through your own perception and beliefs to discover what does work for you. That requires room for independent thought and new ideas. In addition, what works for you with one horse is not necessarily going to work with a different horse. You must develop feel and intuition, think outside the box, be creative, and trust yourself to follow the horse's lead. There are no set rules.

Soulful Horsemanship is not a series of exercises or tools as that would lead to rote performance rather than inspiration. Tools and techniques can run the risk of turning the horse into a machine to perform actions. If you become too focused on applying aids or following the movements prescribed by a technique you can lose track of the feeling and essence of why the aid or exercise was created. Many equestrians get so caught up in the details, results, and specific exercises or methodology that they miss the essence of working with horses – partnership, trust, communication, harmony, balance, and the power of the horse's spirit. Training can sometimes cause people to follow the rules and miss out on the inspiration, energy, and freedom that come from experiencing the horse in the moment. It is better to sit in the silence and allow training to manifest through partnership with the horse. The horse and human come to the arena with their own ideas and ideals and you can take it from there.

Soulful Horsemanship can be used for competition partners, beginner riders, green horses, and non-horse folk through equine facilitated growth and learning. This methodology is about teaching you how to filter all of the information out there on horses and horsemanship through a compassionate lens and right attitude. It is also about teaching you how to develop partnership to unleash power and freedom of the horse and rider. There are no right or wrong answers if you are working with loving kindness. Riding, like life, is not a linear process. Soulful Horsemanship is organic and requires you to be flexible, visit old concepts, and use your skills in different combinations and in different orders. Knowledge comes through your intuition, connection with universal wisdom, and the guidance your horse provides.

If an individual began her riding career within this new framework and perspective she would not have to undo old training and rewire her belief system in the future. This approach is a way forward in the work we do with horses and takes it to a different level. You can still do everything you used to but with new awareness and appreciation. The outcome of this work is the discovery of all of these skills, realizing your potential in the barn and in life, empowering the horse, and expressing your bliss.

Working with the horse is like being in a universal classroom in which you can learn how to build better relationships and how to manifest your desires. Life is all about connection and how we relate to others, the world, and ourselves. Learn to interact with everything in a fulfilling, loving, peaceful, understanding way. Life is also about unleashing your true potential and your deepest desires. With the horse, that may look like riding in harmony, being connected, performing a perfect movement, or having a safe trail ride. It is in your approach and your attitude that you can manifest your desired results without force or coercion. You can create anything if you allow it to flow through you without attachment to the outcome. You can set your life into motion.

When training, you must not get rigid or you will receive rigidity. You must not fight the horse or the horse will fight you. The same is true with the universe. If you want abundance you cannot get there by wishing you weren't poor. You must believe in yourself and feel as though you are already rich and worthy of achieving your goals. The horse acts as a mirror to your inner world, but so does the universe. It is easier to practice your intent, trust, love, bliss, and peace with the direct and immediate feedback of the horse rather than the long and complicated feedback of the universe.

Just because you work through this process with one horse does not mean that you will not gain benefit from working with others in this manner. Each horse has an individual personality, strengths, and weaknesses which can illuminate different issues for you to work through to learn life lessons. For instance, working with a really hot, quick, fiery horse may not bring to the surface an issue with impatience or feeling stuck in your life. However, working with a "kick along" horse that is hard to motivate could uncover those patterns for you.

All of this notwithstanding, I am not suggesting that you should just stand around and be present if working with a dangerous horse. You still need all of the basic knowledge and skill gained from the wisdom of horsemanship. As with all horsemanship, you must be aware of your skill level and the nature of your horse. While typically not the rule, there are some horses that are simply dangerous to work with and they cannot be "fixed". More importantly, there may be some horses that may be dangerous for *you* to work with, depending on your experience and skill. Furthermore, we must all be aware that utilizing a new approach may work to reform a horse but there is no guarantee that Soulful Horsemanship will be successful with every horse. Your safety must always come first.

It is always important to work with horses that fall within your skill level and confidence level. Green horses are better off with experienced riders and vice versa. It is ill informed to put two beginners together because they are both learning and cannot help teach and support the other because they do not yet have the confidence, knowledge, timing, feel, or skill. You do not have third graders teach first graders for a reason.

Change is inevitable. You may have to change your approach with each new horse, and change your strategy as your partnership develops. This is the same with life. A single approach or method will never work for every horse. You must listen and adjust according to your horse's individual needs and your strengths and vulnerabilities. We want to follow a map that someone else drew rather than our own instincts, but if you look within and listen to the feedback from the horse you will be able to shift in the moment and have a fluid experience. If we get stuck on specific exercises or equipment as promoted by someone, then we can no longer use our universal wisdom to walk our own path. If we look for quick fix solutions we end up with gadgets, such as draw reins and spurs, that can result in a hollow, empty shell of a horse. If, instead, we trust ourselves, we can work through the process and foster fulfillment and empowerment for the horse and human. You can't always have the answers without the work to attain them.

A rider often describes or explains a training issue based on what the horse is or is not doing, rather than what she, the human, is or is not doing. We often place blame on the horse. "My horse is refusing ditches" instead of "I have a fear of ditches". You are the only one that you can control, so frame training issues in terms of yourself. What can you change within your heart and soul? Work on that, and more often than not, the horse will reflect your change.

By changing our perspective, we change our beliefs and actions, which ultimately change our reality. You can use training principles in your life by working to be a little better, a little more aware, and a little more powerful each day. With the horse, you continue to do your best and make small changes one day at a time and the horse will continue to lead you down your path and reveal your soul to you. Don't get stuck in all the details. Trust yourself, the horse, the universe, and the process.

Building a partnership

Often riders are so focused on their discipline that they miss the essence of the magical experience of working with horses. We tend to have laser vision to learn the techniques necessary to be proficient at trail riding, jumping, reining, dressage, or barrel racing that we forget that we are working with an amazing, beautiful animal. Learning those skills should be a joyous game, an activity to do with your partner, but it is the development of the partnership that is the sweetest.

If you were forming a friendship you wouldn't just go hiking in silence trying to climb bigger and bigger mountains to the exclusion of doing anything else together. You would go hiking if both of you enjoyed the activity and, along the way you would talk, bond, laugh, and build the friendship. You would also go to dinner, see a movie, or sit and talk over coffee. It should be no different with the horse. You should enjoy each other's company and design every task to not simply get better at it, but to enrich your lives and deepen the quality of your partnership.

Relationship is the center of your work together. The magic happens where the horse and human overlap. It is important to fully care for the horse and the self at the same time so that you are surrounding the relationship with care, love, and well-being. In this way you can heal the horse and human alike. You can connect on all levels. The effort that is made, and the changes initiated through your partnership, will have a ripple effect on the rest of the world. At the intersection of the horse and human is a connection on an energetic, emotional, soul-based level that can lead to wholeness, self-awareness, and personal development. When you create balance and live from a state of love it affects the entire universe. Now is the time to trust yourself and begin unfolding the process of right relationship with your horse.

The concepts that fill the remaining chapters build the base of Soulful Horsemanship techniques that will lead to the vision we created for empowered partnership and emotional freedom. The process starts with you. Your body, mind, and soul are the base on which the partnership is formed. You only have control over yourself. The change you can effect in others comes as a reflection of the changes you make in yourself. Your body and mind are linked by your emotions and create the base of your experience in this life.

Traditional methods build the pillars that support all of your training and riding. You develop your body through balance, body mechanics, body language, and applying aids. You also develop your mind through knowledge, theory, and understanding of training principles. The body and mind rely on one another, and if one is off it affects the other. Holes in either or both impact your ability to communicate effectively with the horse. The soul connects the physical and mental through emotional, energetic messages. Soulful Horsemanship methods will help fill in the gaps in your physical and mental structures and glue those together by focusing on your heart and soul.

Once you create your base you can move into the feelings of love, belonging, friendship, and connection. There is room to build self-esteem, confidence, compassion, respect of self and others, and start to value the unique individuality of you and your horse. From that space you can work on overcoming fear, forgiving yourself and others, and developing the confidence in your ability to work with the horse in a new intuitive manner. Personal insight is paired with reworking your horse and seeing the training process in a new light to develop mutual trust.

You will start to play with your horse and learn to erase your preconceived notions of how to relate with one another. Then you will let that settle in by becoming still and interacting in the present moment. You will have the opportunity to delve into your awareness of body, mind, and soul This process is not about driving yourself forward to the achievement of new goals – it is about observing the horse, centering yourself, working on the basics, and experiencing everything.

Your partnership will continue to develop through the mutual trust that comes from clear communication. You will work on learning to use intuition and intention to communicate in a mutually beneficial manner that provides your horse with a voice and reduces your reliance on physical means to gain results. As you develop intuition, awareness, and communication you will both continue to develop, learn, and listen.

Once communication is established you can begin to have a positive effect on the horse's body, mind, and emotions. Then you can begin to lead the horse to his own betterment of skills in your chosen discipline. This is the area that leads to the development of specific training for your discipline. However, you will continue to use new, soulful means to effectively lead your horse to his highest potential while maintaining his freedom and allowing his voice to be heard.

This communication in turn leads to the development of purpose for horse and human, and the work begins to have a more focused intent in which you both find your power and bliss. You both start to feel good and spontaneously express your joy. You begin working as one in harmony, helping you to train your horse as a riding or competition partner. Your journey to attain a harmonious partnership with your horse is also symbolic of your path as a soul through life. You can shift from feeling disempowered and separate, unable to realize your dreams, to a state of connectedness, fulfillment, vitality, authenticity, playfulness, creativity, acceptance, mastery, recognition, and self-actualization.

The horse can lead you to unlocking your purpose in life, allowing you to look through new eyes to express and manifest your highest self. You can begin to live in peace and harmony while vibrating in tune with yourself, the horse, and the universe. You can open yourself to overwhelming happiness that makes you want to live, share, and find the freedom that leads to the expression of light and love. The work will also allow the horse to find ways to express himself through freedom of movement. Both of you develop the ability to create and manifest your dreams through intense positive energy and co-create a new experience and way of working

The Soulful Horsemanship Pyramid

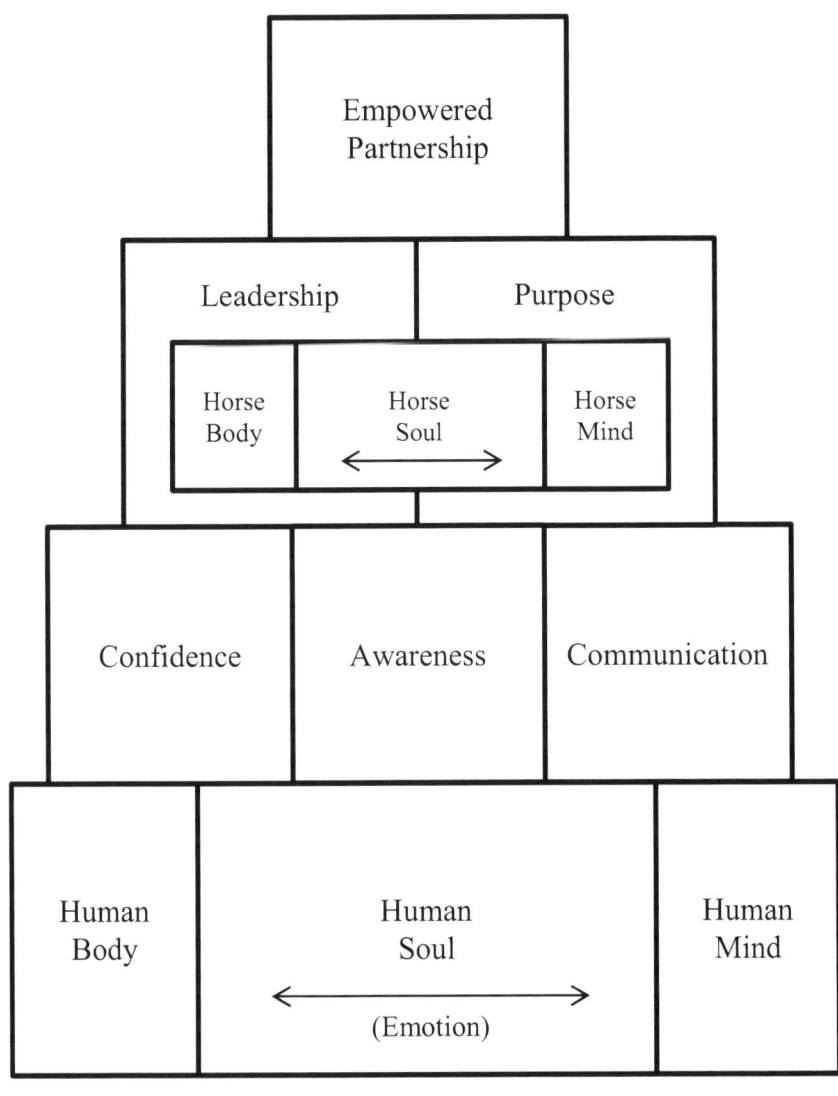

together. By changing your perspective you can actively create your reality.

Through self-actualization you no longer need to defend your identity. You can have a very simple, joyful partnership that leads both of you to greatness. You can let go of training gimmicks and gadgets devised for manipulation and control because you are working in unity with the horse. You will find peace in yourself and your partnership and work in a state of respect and collaboration. Transcend the old you and transform into an empowered being while encouraging the horse to do the same. The sky becomes the limit.

Inspiration and creativity will be abundant and lead the two of you to new heights. The world will begin to look a little different for both of you. You will hear and know your true self. You can live in service with humility and graciousness. Through Soulful Horsemanship you build a genuine connection where both horse and human are empowered, opinionated, and expressive. It is a true partnership in which both contribute and reap the benefits. Those benefits are carried out of the arena into the rest of your life through enlightenment and a connection to spirit.

Spiritual development in the barn

Working with the horse can be a spiritual experience that helps you to live a heart centered life that heals you on a soul level. Healing yourself is the greatest gift you can give humanity. There are themes throughout spiritual practices that help you live a more soul centered, enlightened, joyful life. The horse can reveal all of these practices to you as you work through the concepts laid out in the remaining chapters. They include:

- Learning to be clear in your intention
- Quieting your mind
- Communicating effectively and listening
- Living with gratitude
- Trusting
- Releasing attachment to outcomes & worldly possessions
- Becoming defenseless in your position
- Building confidence through self-worth and self-love
- Connecting with others
- Finding purpose
- Listening to intuition
- Connecting to the moment
- Surrendering
- Acting with honesty and integrity
- Living with loving kindness
- Acting with compassion and empathy
- Unlocking your true potential and the possibilities in life
- Overcoming fear
- Stepping into the light
- Becoming aware
- Forgiving
- Releasing harmful patterns
- Being responsible
- Practicing non-judgment and acceptance
- Putting forth your best effort through right action
- Living with grace
- Finding balance
- Acknowledging your true desires
- Giving and receiving love
- Serving others
- Unlocking your creativity
- Living with reverence for everything
- Recognizing the interconnectedness of the universe
- Embracing the perfection of the moment

All of these practices are potential pathways to a more fulfilling life. They hold the divine wisdom to lead you to a conscientious life filled with joy, love, and peace. These are things taught by religion and spiritual practices all over the world but you can embrace all of them in the barn. If you work on mastery of the self, the soul, the mind, and the body while at the barn you can carry that power and wisdom with you through life. You can improve the entirety of your life including your relationships and career. You can find freedom. You cannot change your life without first surrendering. Let go of all your preconceived notions and the need to be right, to be in control, to be approved of, and let the horse carry you to a new perspective.

Sometimes people run so hard toward something that they run right past what they really want. We think that when we get the new job or the blue ribbon or our horse is finally cutting cattle that we will feel satisfied and it will bring us happiness. We focus so hard on getting there with such determination that we forget to experience the process of transformation that is required for us to arrive at that point. Once we achieve those goals we aren't guaranteed happiness and fulfillment. It is the path, and all of the stepping stones along the way, that hold the key to happiness. When you arrive at the end goal, you will feel the way that you did coming into it. If you feel empty and as though you are striving for more on your journey there, you will feel empty and striving for more when you get there. If you feel joyful, grateful, and satisfied on your path, you will feel joyful, grateful, and satisfied at your destination.

Don't run past all the work and opportunities for a happy life thinking that some end goal will solve all of your problems. Don't get stuck in the pursuit of happiness. Happiness can only be had now, not at some point in the future. Step into that happiness by becoming congruent and pulling together the self, body, mind, and soul, with your greater worldly concerns, whatever they may be, to resonate as one in the interconnectedness of everything. Forgiveness, understanding, collaboration, compassion, love, and truth resonate with all that is. Live in the light.

The work that we do with horses can lead us from being no one, to know one, to now one, and back to no one. We begin our spiritual journey as no one with the perception that we are nothingness because we have no self-love, self-worth, or self-respect. We do not yet know our power and purpose. We are the unrealized human. We live in a world tied to what happened, what might happen, worrying what others will think, attached to the material world, needing more, wanting more, judging others, struggling, striving, stressed, overwhelmed, unhappy, never present, with the ego calling out the battle cry of "me, me, me!" Our lives are ego-driven and lonely because we are isolated in our own mini networks of people scrambling through life trying to attain something that we hope will make us happy. We are in need of recognition from others in order to recognize ourselves.

From there we shift to know one. We start to become aware of our higher selves and our calling through meditation, self-growth, and the reflection of the horse. We start to become aware of who we really are. We are a soul having a physical experience and not the persona that is created by the ego. We begin to work on releasing the labels, forgiving others, living in the moment, awakening to our power while letting go of our attachment to the material world, the needing, wanting, grasping, pleading, begging, and striving. We can stop our attempts to predict the future, change the past, and control everything. We go through a process of releasing and surrendering the egocentric thought patterns and delve into the light of the heart and soul.

Next we move to now one. We start to fully live in the present moment for that is all we have. We start to feel the interconnectedness of everything that is. We come to understand that life is not about me versus them. It is about us. Without all of us, the good and the bad, none of us could exist. It does us no good to try to rise above others because we are one and the same. Instead, raise others up and we too will be lifted. We must all work together. We only have this moment that we are in right now to make the choice to help us all. We are all part of the divine and have the power to contribute to the healing of humanity.

As we embrace this perception, we are able to shift back into a sense of being no one. Now we realize that we are not insignificant. We understand that we hold an enormous amount of power but we no longer need things and others to recognize or validate us. We begin to live with a sense of humility and grace. We now live in a state of harmonious energy and are connected through the heart to everything in the universe. We are no longer some*body* having an experience. We are now spirit reveling in the amazing experience of physical form. Through that understanding we can rise above the physical realm all together as one.

How can the horse teach you these types of profound lessons? You learn them through approaching problems with a new outlook. Let's look at a common horse training difficulty, loading a resistant horse into the trailer, as an example of the way that you could change your approach and learn insight about yourself. The horse's actions are likely an authentic reaction, based on his instinctual claustrophobia, to keep himself safe and do what is in his best interest. However, you could perceive or judge your horse's actions as stubborn or willful which would make you frustrated and lead to forceful tactics. This situation provides you with an opportunity to stop, bring awareness to your thoughts, and ask yourself about how you are feeling. Why are you interpreting his behavior in that way?

The things we wish to change in others are often a reflection of the things we need to change in ourselves. So if you perceive the horse as acting stubborn or willful your horse is really holding up a mirror to reflect that perception. Ask yourself, in what areas are you stubbornly denying yourself or imposing your will on others? It's not about the horse's behavior; it's about your beliefs. Life is all about perception and the way we view our circumstances. This gives you a chance to see how you can go with the flow in this situation and in life. How can you cooperate and let go of your stubborn, willful attitude that the horse must do what you're asking?

Become aware of what you are resisting and decide whether or not you want to let go of it. If so, ask yourself, "What is happening right now?" Move into your heart space and feel your emotions and the sensations in your body. Don't judge what you find or look for specific answers. Just allow what is there to make itself known. Then ask, "Can I just let that be?" Can you embrace your feelings without an agenda and just feel them? Think about who you want to be and be that person now. You are that person. Feel it.

By turning the situation back on yourself, you can then change your approach, becoming creative in discovering new ways to perceive the problem, and figuring out how to help the horse be successful at the task at hand. And guess what? As you change your perception and approach the horse with cooperation, understanding, and compassion, the horse will mirror you. Now success can unfold in time. You have addressed your issue, and the horse's issue, and can proceed with a new attitude. This will often allow the issue to just melt away. Your life will only change when you decide to change it. Surrender to the power of the universe and soul rather than forcing your life into small constraints.

Creative problem solving to benefit training

Soulful Horsemanship is about feeling your emotions, examining your beliefs, and generating a sense of who you are, but you can also use this philosophy in a very practical manner to meet your training needs. Let's say you are having trouble getting your horse to yield his shoulders. Yielding the shoulders, or a turn on the haunches, requires the horse to step sideways with the front legs while pivoting around the hind end. A problem performing this maneuver could be an issue in the horse, the human, or the partnership. Traditionally, trainers teach a specific method for each movement in training based on what works for them. Or maybe they give you a specific tool that they like. It is possible that their technique or tool will work to solve the problem for you, but you run the risk of mechanizing the experience. In addition, each horse/human partnership is unique and may require a different approach.

If I were to give you a solution for yielding the shoulders, I have not taught you to problem solve, use creative thinking, follow your intuition, and work through the problem in an organic way. If, instead, you are given the parameters of the problem and guided to solve it on your own then you will be able to solve other problems as they arise. Rather than learning that 2 + 2 = 4 and memorizing it, you can be taught the math so that you can answer other arithmetic problems. That way you don't have to rely on someone telling you what 3 + 7 equals. You will know how to add those numbers together to find the answer on your own. I could teach you an answer for each problem that arises without providing a solution because I could have the equation wrong. I am not part of your partnership with your horse.

In other words, rather than giving you an answer to memorize, I can teach you to break the problem down into its component parts and then help teach you to solve the equation on your own. If yielding the shoulders is the equivalent to the number 5, there is more than one arithmetic equation to arrive at the answer. I may break it down as $2 + 3 = 5$ but for your unique partnership maybe the steps to get there are $4 + 1 = 5$, or $1 + 3 + 1 = 5$, or $1 + 1 + 1 + 1 + 1 = 5$. To yield the shoulders effectively, you need to find the pieces that work for you and your horse as a team to get the desired results. You need to develop an understanding that the shoulders are the heaviest and most difficult part of the body for the horse to move and that there are many possibilities to help him learn this skill based on your cue.

You may realize that any of the following paths are possibilities for unlocking this skill with your horse. This is by no means an exhaustive list:

- o Your horse needs to first shift his weight to his hind end before the shoulders are free. In that case you may start by backing to teach him to shift his weight back. Then you can use a subtle shift backward so the horse can step sideways with the front end.
- o Your horse is not stuck in his shoulder at all, but in his hind end. You may try yielding the haunches first and later return to the shoulders.
- o Your horse hasn't figured out to isolate one part of his body. So you could try starting with side pass and then shift into moving sideways with just the shoulder.
- o Your horse is stuck because he standing still, in which case you could start by walking forward and turning the horse away from you until the circle gets small enough that he pivots around his hind end.
- o Your horse understands moving toward you but not away from you so you could try bringing the shoulder toward you to develop an understanding to then move it away from you.

- You discover that your horse does not understand your current cue and you need a whip, or other form of pointer, to channel your energy and make your intention clearer so the horse can grasp the nature of the request.
- You discover that you are cueing at the shoulder because that is the part that you want to move but your horse is more sensitive and responsive to pressure applied at his neck.
- You become aware that you are holding tension in your shoulders and your horse is mirroring you. Therefore, you must relax so the horse can relax and yield.

Those are eight possible equations to get to the number 5, or yielding the shoulders. This is why you can't get caught up in the methodology. Work through each problem based on you and your horse's unique partnership, strengths, and weaknesses. If you just assume the horse is stubborn, demand that he yield, and continue increasing the pressure until he complies, then you miss out on all the good stuff. Sure, you may get what you want faster but at what cost? Sometimes the best way to get a result is by doing something else. What are the component parts of the desired end result? Practice those pieces and then come back to the bigger puzzle.

It is also important to remember that when you finally get that step sideways it is time to praise the horse and move on. Don't keep drilling the horse. Give it time to sink in and come back to it another day. A behavior is better reinforced by ending on a good, short note than over-doing it. Go do something else and when you come back to it tomorrow start with the exercise that unlocked the problem. He will get it more quickly this time and you can ask him to take a few more steps. Then let go of it again. You gradually, over time, increase the amount you ask for in small increments until you have an effortless turn on the haunches.

Also remember that what your horse learns on one side does not automatically translate to the other side. Don't become frustrated. Simply work through the problem on the other side and continue to reward any effort. Much like humans, horses tend to have a dominant and weak side. It is often easier to teach a behavior on his good side but when you practice the skill you will work slightly more often on the weak side to build strength and keep him balanced. If you were teaching a right-handed child to write and you wanted her to be ambidextrous, you would teach her each letter with first the right hand and then the left. Once she knew the letter she would need to practice it on both hands but would need to dedicate a bit more time with the left because it is more challenging. Perhaps a 40/60 split.

Horses will sometimes take what you teach them on one side and attempt to translate it on the other with difficulty. They are not good at this. For example, when my horse, Radar, was learning to leg yield, he figured out how to leg yield to the right with no trouble. When I applied the aids to leg yield left, he would leg yield right. None of our training had ever said move into my leg pressure, but he just couldn't quite figure it out. That is not the time to punish him, get frustrated, call him stupid, kick him a little harder, or smack him with a whip. Those things would be unnecessarily punitive since he was offering a behavior and trying to understand. Those things may have gotten the desired results, but he wouldn't have been given a chance to learn, figure it out, and assimilate the information.

Radar got frustrated because he was trying to give me the correct response but I was not releasing the pressure. I also wasn't adding pressure because he was in fact leg yielding, but releasing the pressure would have rewarded him for the wrong response. As a sensitive horse I could feel him trying to work it out, get stuck, and fall into one of his old avoidance behaviors. He put his head straight up and started to scoot away. Okay. I let him move forward, let him calm down and relax, and tried again. If I had fought back or blocked him from moving off, it would have escalated the situation and created an environment that is not conducive to learning. With this particular horse, he would have tried bucking to get rid of the person who wouldn't release the pressure.

When I went back to the problem, leg yield left, we hit the same wall. He remembered leg yield right and gave it to me even though that wasn't what I wanted. This time I realized I needed a different approach. He already knew turn on the forehand and haunches in both directions. So we did two steps turn on the forehand then two steps turn on the haunches and moved like a sidewinder to the left. We continued to work the problem in short increments until we got to the point that I would ask for leg yield left, he would shift his weight to the right, and I would immediately change my cue to shoulder left one step, haunches left one step – and then the light bulb turned on. We got two steps leg yield left – woohoo! I let him canter off – a special reward, since he loved thundering around the arena – ecstatically praising him. And then we called it a day.

I would then ask, almost every ride, for a little leg yield at some point to solidify the concept. I would typically start with the left and end with the left with some right leg yield thrown in for balance. Once he got it he never lost it because he was given a chance to work through the problem and learn it on his own without stress. Remember that everything you teach your horse needs to have meaning, purpose, and serve as a means to help empower the horse.

For Radar, leg yield turned into one of his favorite moves. It became a "sanctioned" escape valve for him. He was a very spooky horse and his form of spooking was the snort, spin, and run away method. I became aware that he would bend his body away from an object for a split second before the snort and spin. Aha! I captured that bend and would ask for leg yield away from the goblin in the shadows. It gave him a way to concentrate on me and his body rather than unravel into panic. It gave him permission to move away from the threat and ultimately left him feeling calm and successful. We would leg yield away, travel straight for a few steps and then leg yield back over to my intended path, whether that was on the rail in the arena or trail out cross country. We had a couple of rides where we must have looked inebriated travelling through the cow field, leg yielding this way and that. Eventually something started to shift. He was starting to spook less and less.

I was giving him permission to have his spook in a controlled manner, he was no longer high tailing it out of there, and the panic lessened because he not yet been harmed by the threat or punished by the rider on his back. He was starting to trust me and his confidence grew. He never stopped spooking entirely, but he got to the point he would move sideways a couple steps on his own, think it through, move back over, and continue down trail with his head on his shoulders. It gave him an outlet and way to feel safe and empowered. It gave me an opportunity to grow, learn, and develop confidence. In addition, it was a mutually beneficial process that left both of us feeling great about our rides together and allowed us to connect in a magnificent manner.

This is what we want. Schooling that has greater usefulness than just surrendering to commands the horse doesn't understand for the temporary pleasure of the rider. We can realize the life of our dreams while cantering off into the sunset on our empowered partner. Use the process of training the horse, and his development, as a means to attain your own self-actualization. Look at horses to dive into the truth in your heart. See your horse's power and energy as a reflection of that which is within you and unleash your magnificence. Are you ready for the journey?

Chapter Three:
Compassionate Confidence

Compassion: *sympathetic consciousness of other's distress together with a desire to alleviate it*
Confidence: *faith that one will act in a right, proper or effective way; a feeling of one's powers*

Your journey to empowered partnership begins by unraveling your prior training and conditioning in order to create a space for growth and learning. You must start by detaching from the outcome to allow the process to unfold. Find a way to surrender to the moment and trust that the universe will carry you. Begin to heal yourself through unconditional love and self-worth to allow your true essence to emerge. Develop a well of compassion to see where both you and the horse are struggling and foster a deep desire to alleviate that stress. Allow the power within you to create the drive to move confidently toward the life of your dreams. Rather than trying to leverage power and control over the horse you can let go and assist him to express himself authentically on his journey through life. This unraveling of truth is necessary for the horse and human alike to build the confidence required to step into an empowered partnership.

In order to fully surrender and detach from the outcomes of training we must see the limiting beliefs that keep us locked into a feeling of grasping for control. The root of limitation is a fear-based life. When we make decisions based out of fear we are in a constant state of resistance because we are trying to avoid pain. As long as we fear the possible outcomes of our actions we can never fully surrender. We are afraid of failure *and* success. We are afraid of not having enough or not being good enough. We are afraid of our internal experiences and feelings, leading to self-doubt. We are afraid of our external experiences and circumstances, leading to insecurity. As long as we feel as though we are not worthy and do not belong we will never be capable of making the lasting changes that lead to a fulfilling life.

Shifting from fear to love

Let's look at the fear that stems from your past and the unknown to build the confidence to begin working toward a partnership and life that is based in love. This is done by developing compassion for yourself and the horse, wiping the slate clean, and building new experiences based on a trusting relationship. There is a lot of fear in riding for the horse and human. Much of it comes from moving too quickly, before one or both are ready. Working with a horse gives you a chance to overcome your fears while also helping the horse overcome his. You can't necessarily get rid of fear. Acting courageously is about acknowledging and accepting your fear and choosing to believe in yourself in spite of it.

Fear is not a demon that we should resist. If we resist it we will become afraid of the fear itself. In reality, it is a natural emotion designed to keep us physically safe. We must learn how to listen to the message when it is acting in our best interest and how to shift that message when it is based on old, limiting beliefs. The only way to do this is to fully experience the fear and allow it to flow through us. We must understand the ways in which it works to utilize its wisdom. This emotion shows up in our body as flight, fight, or freeze. While this is useful if you are about to become dinner for a bear it is not so helpful if you are trying to step into your power.

For example, let's say that in order to make your dream in life come true you need to write a grant to get funding for your project.

Fear may show up based on an uncertainty about the future – "What if I don't get the money? What if I fail?" That apprehension may be based on your past – "My last business failed. I never get what I want." Those are limiting beliefs that cause you to give up on your dream (flight), resist the process (fight), or become incapable of moving past this hurdle (freeze). The only way to get from here to your dream is by changing your beliefs, practicing new behavior patterns, and surrendering to the wisdom in your heart.

Fear leads us to make decisions to avoid getting hurt. We try to stay safe and protect ourselves. From this line of thinking we make decisions that ultimately fail because we don't move toward the vision of our dreams. We are no longer living in alignment with our true calling and therefore we cannot find happiness and fulfillment. Over time it becomes even harder to follow the call of our soul and the stirrings in our heart because we have been practicing failure and living a small, unsuccessful, unfulfilled life. We choose not to persist in our pursuit of our dreams, further reinforcing the belief system that we are unworthy or incapable.

Telling yourself that you are stupid, a baby, a sissy, or any other chiding remark in response to fear does nothing to deal with the under lying cause. Positive affirmations also don't deal with the problem – they just mask it without diving into the root of it. What is the basis of your fear? Is it "legitimate" fear that is going to keep you safe or is it founded on the pack of lies your ego tells you about how you are not good enough? Trust yourself so that you can listen to your fear and choose how to best respond. Keep yourself grounded and see if you can transform your fear into fulfillment. You can't always stay comfortable if you want to achieve big dreams. You must face the fear so that you can break out of the pattern and step into a love-based life. Through love we can make decisions that will make us feel wonderful.

A love-based life is all about seeking pleasure and embracing life. We all need to be loved and feel understood but do you know what love really feels like? I was once asked how we know that spirit is within us and I answered that it is a feeling of love. This wise woman followed up with the question "and what does love feel like?" I sat there stunned in front of a room full of people without a single definition.

I realized that the reason I couldn't answer that question had nothing to do with whether other people loved me. The truth is I didn't love myself. Until we learn to love and accept ourselves we cannot accept love from others or truly love others. Love and pleasure have a much higher vibration than fear and displeasure but few people live in this state. If we can learn to make decisions based on what feels good and right to us we will find our path and success – however you may define success for yourself. We can do away with the stress that is the result of resisting our current state and living out of alignment with our true desires and purpose. As a result of choosing to make that shift I feel love, not fear, in everything I do.

We will approach this process by asking ourselves: what do we have, what do we love, and for what are we grateful? We have the awesome opportunity to work with horses we love and appreciate. We can build reverence for ourselves out of that relationship. We can practice loving kindness. Divine love is without ego and is not conditioned on having another life to possess – it is about loving everything and everyone for who and what they are. Unconditional love and self-love hinge on the act of forgiveness. Forgiveness acts like a healing salve for the soul and allows us to overcome troubling emotions. One of the kindest things we can do for ourselves is to forgive ourselves and others. If we can't forgive someone, who are we hurting more – us or them?

Having compassion for ourselves involves understanding that we have been doing our best with our life based on our perspective. This includes our work with horses. We have been following the methods that are widely known and accepted. With that acknowledgment we can find new ways to live life and relate to the horse. We can let go of the external and turn into ourselves. We can step into bigger shoes and take our life and our time in the barn to the next level. We can soar. Now is not the time to blame ourselves – it is time to approach work with the horse in an enlightened way. Now is the time to stop searching for what is lacking, what we resist, and what we wish was different and start embracing the experience.

Perfectionism is a common thing to face in training, but we can develop a new definition of what it means to be perfect. Traditionally it has meant that we strive for something better because we feel that we are not good enough and do not stack up to others – both in comparison to others and in meeting the expectations that others have for us. We struggle with a desire to be the best rather than to do our best. We place that standard onto the horse as well, with an assumption that they are not good enough, that we need to fix them, and mold them into something better. We can let go of this definition to see the innate perfection in everything – ourselves, our actions, our horses, our training, and the unfolding of each moment.

All horses are already perfect as they are. They are on their own path. We can support our horses in their development without imposing our limitations onto them. If we allow each horse to be true to himself, he can reflect his beauty and wisdom on us, allowing each of us to see that we are also perfect as we are. There is always room for growth and expansion but we must meet ourselves with love in the moment. From there we can see that the things we were labeling as imperfect are actually the perfect opportunity for us to learn. For example, if we struggle motivating a horse what does that say about our inner world? How can we work to overcome that and gain something positive? Where do we need to be motivated in our own lives? This is not a fault with the horse but an opportunity for us.

Allow the horse to be who he is, support him on his journey, and learn from him. We are attracted to certain horses for the ways that they can help us. We create struggle and conflict with the horse by not accepting him as he is. We feel that we must train him, make him behave, teach him to respect us as his master, and obey our commands. From now on we can choose to accept his gifts of being a horse, acting like a horse, and expressing himself as a horse. If we look for what he can teach us we will no longer feel the need to battle with him which causes suffering for everyone. Learn to accept what is and allow the process to unfold.

Only you can be an expert on you – you are the only one having the experience of you. No one knows what it is like to look through your eyes, feel with your fingers, or laugh with your joy. Others can make suggestions as to what they think would help you in life but you are the only one who knows what feels good and right to you so you must trust yourself.

Why would it be any different for the horse? How can we be an expert of his experience? We are not in his body. In fact, we are not even the same species. So all we can do is make suggestions as to what we think would be helpful and it is up to the horse to decide if it is. It is his choice, his experience. We must respect and honor that, offer multiple suggestions from which to choose, and provide support for him to find his own solution.

Allowing authenticity

Start wherever you are with your horse and meet him as he is. Begin simply by opening an awareness to watch the interaction between you. See if you can surrender slightly in your interactions. If you feel that you are not ready, start by watching your horse at a distance. We will not just march up to the horse with a halter and declare it is time to work and follow the human's rules. Begin to see the possibility that the horse can be your teacher. What wisdom or lesson does your horse have for you today? When we approach the horse with this attitude we can learn a lot about ourselves.

By allowing the horse to have freedom of choice we open up to possibilities that we may have never conceived of on our own. By giving up all that was we create a space for what we thought was not possible to grow and become a reality. We will start this process of allowance on the ground and at a distance. We will start by observing the horse and how he responds to our presence. Experiment to see what happens if you do different things, such as changing your mood, thoughts, energy, or intention. We will also become aware of how we respond to the horse. Notice what arises within you in response to your horses actions.

Literally and figuratively let go and trust the horse to make decisions. Let him figure stuff out on his own without nagging him about every little step. We can provide support and direction when needed but this is a chance to stay out of his way, let him be expressive, and make his own decisions. When we hold on too tight we end up strangling the things we love. A lack of openness to learn and try new approaches doesn't leave room for inspired creativity. No longer will we approach the horse thinking "my way is *the* way". The horse has thoughts, opinions, ideas, and feelings that we will respect. No longer will we act condescending and assume the horse needs us to show him every little thing. Give him responsibility for himself and encourage his ingenuity.

The horse is a magnificent creature but if we rob him of his liberty he can no longer shine bright. We need to go from selfish to selfless focusing on our commonalities rather than on our differences. It is time to become conscious of our choices and responsible for our actions. We no longer need to limit the horse or ourselves. We must approach this process with defenselessness – we can't always be right. To find the horse's motivation we must also let go of our judgments and preconceived ideas so that both can enter the arena with vulnerability and sensitivity. Go wherever you and your horse take yourselves – don't worry about rushing it. This is a leap of faith for horse and human.

Approach the horse with non-attachment. If we aren't locked in to a specified outcome we may get different – or even better – results. Relationships, including the partnership with the horse, will fall apart as soon as you become attached to expectations because expectations cause judgment and control issues. We can be happy regardless of how the horse chooses to respond. Don't take it personally. Others are free to be themselves, act according to their thoughts and feelings, follow their inclinations based on their desires, and behave in ways that are suitable to them, just as you are free to be yourself. Remain neutral in response to your horse without the need to become irritated by or prideful of his actions. Your horse's antics just are, good or bad, and all you need to do is stay engaged without the need to win at all cost.

Horses are masters of truth and can teach you how to live a more honest, open, confident life. Start noticing how horses react to different people, horses, and stimuli in their environment. Watch without trying to manipulate the situation. Horses are incapable of lying so there is no reason not to trust them. Through observation you will start to see that they always respond authentically. They may not do what a person is asking but their undesirable behavior is most often due to a misunderstanding, fear, or an honest reaction to the person's energy or attitude. They are not capable of the thought process required to be vindictive. Therefore, behavior that is labeled as 'bad' is actually an honest reaction based on how they are feeling.

Horses do not mask their emotions. If they want another horse to get out of their space or move away from the trough they simply push the other horse away with clear intent. They do not manipulate or devise a story about why they want the horse to move – they just communicate how they feel. They act in a way that is true to their heart. Pushing a horse away doesn't come with "I don't like you", "you're not good enough" or "I'm better than you". They simply stand up for themselves and what they need. It also isn't read by the other horse as a rejection.

Horses simply "speak" the truth and do what is going to fulfill them in that moment. They can choose to play with or groom another horse – or not. Choosing not to participate doesn't mean they close the door to doing it later when that would feel good. The same is true for you when you are working with horses. You have the choice to say no or move a horse out of your space. If it is done with calm intent based on your needs it is not offensive to the horse.

Once you assert yourself let it go and resist the desire to hold onto the need to keep asserting yourself. And don't feel bad for creating those boundaries. Both horse and human should be able to make the decision that something isn't working for you and there is no implicit rejection in your behavior. Learning to speak the truth can carry over into the world. Stand up for yourself when necessary and let go of trying to be something other than who you are. Express yourself fairly and honestly.

Humans are the only creatures who try to be something they are not. Think of all the damage that is caused by not being honest with yourself. Most of us are not even honest with ourselves about our thoughts and emotions. We act according to what we think we should do or what others want us to do rather than following our hearts. The horse can teach you to be congruent and authentic, to live your truth, to live on purpose, and to be as awesome as you are. Everything in the natural world is what it is without trying to be something different. Therefore, you always know where you stand with horses because they have no hidden agendas.

The horse will look at your actions, sense your energy, and know who you really are. If you are angry, annoyed, or frustrated that you can't catch your horse, for example, but are trying to mask it with your behavior the horse can't fathom it. He reads the tension in your body and sees the predator in you. Though you are trying to act friendly and coy on the surface the horse will simply read that as you stalking him. Don't give your horse a chance to not trust you. Be authentic, kind, and trustworthy while emanating love and compassion. If you are not there yet at least be honest about what you are feeling and work through it.

Horses do not judge us, call us wrong, or automatically reject us. What they respect and listen to are honesty, integrity, and authenticity. They respond to us in the moment and will connect when we find our authentic power. You cannot doubt yourself. Working with the horse is about more than tools and techniques – it is about who you are and your presence, actions, thoughts, and emotions. The horse will not judge you or push you away for being who you are and feeling your emotions. It is when you are false that he becomes uneasy because, in the moment, you are projecting a lie.

Horses don't think about whom they should trust; they sense it. This means that we must do two things to communicate trustworthiness: be congruent and honest about who you are and what you are feeling; and learn to connect on the level of feeling rather than thinking. We need to move out of our head and ego and into the heart and soul. We tend to cast aside our instinctual, intuitive feeling in favor of logical, linear thinking. If we learn to connect and communicate from the heart we can eventually develop mutual trust.

We can work with the horse as a creative endeavor to practice skills that will be helpful to us in life. We cannot give our horse, or anyone else, that which we don't have. We have to learn to be honest with ourselves. We must be dependable and trustworthy. We reap what we sow throughout life. Therefore, whatever we give to the horse we will receive in return. If you want a reliable, willing partner, be a reliable, willing partner; if you want the horse to listen, listen; if you want trust, trust; if you want compliance, comply; if you want honesty, be honest; if you want courage, be courageous.

Going back to basics

We can learn a lot through observation and allowing the horse to act authentically. Eventually we are going to want to do more than notice what is happening. Before we can begin moving forward, everyone would benefit from going through the process of wiping the slate clean. It is time to let go of the grip the past has on our lives and accept it for what it is. The beliefs we have created around our memories affect our actions, reactions, and inactions in life. Any negative expression or energy that is holding us back can be converted into a positive expression if we are willing to release its grip on us, forgive, and be grateful for the lessons it brought. If we stop complaining we can start being thankful and celebrate the events in our lives that have brought us to where we are. In order to move forward in new directions we must unravel the results of the past to stand on neutral ground with the horse.

Through compassion we can show the horse that we are going to start interacting in a new way. We need the horse to see that, from now on, they are going to be heard and that our work together is going to have a new purpose. We are going to unlock the horse's power and encourage him to join us on this new path with enthusiasm. This process will benefit horse and human alike but we must take the initiative and lead the process with flexibility. The horse does not yet know what he is going to gain. Many horses live in a state of disassociation that comes from not being able to flee from danger or a threat. Some horses that are seen as submissive, cooperative, or even a willing partner are not at all – they have disassociated or shut down to protect themselves.

We owe it to them to break through that state of closing themselves off. It has come from our training methods and attitudes. When we work with a horse and enter his personal space or touch him we expect, even require, that he will consent. However, when our horse enters our space we consider it disrespectful and push him away. This type of behavior does not make sense. It is not fair and empowering. Furthermore, if we don't feel like riding we don't go to the barn. If we go anyway it is our choice because we believe it will make us feel better. We need the same to be true for the horse. He can determine if it would be beneficial and, if not, he has the right to do something else. That is not disobedience – that is the horse deciding what is best for him.

This is not to say that you should let your horse walk all over you or condone bad behavior. Defenselessness, love, and respect do not mean that you allow someone else to harm you, push you around, or make you uncomfortable. While you do not want to judge the horse when he makes decisions the goal is mutual trust and respect which naturally leads to understanding and accepting one another's boundaries. Safety always comes first but there is a big difference between creating boundaries and punishing the horse based on demands he does not understand. If you want the horse to have manners you must also have manners. If you want the horse to respect your boundaries you must also respect his. This may require working within his time line and comfort zone. Patience is your greatest tool as you allow the process to unfold.

It is important to set clear expectations around potentially dangerous behavior like biting. You can establish personal boundaries without violating the horse or acting restrictive. It isn't mean to claim your space. You do not have to beg and plead with the horse. You own your bubble and that should be respected unless you invite him in. The same has to be true for the horse. Don't get so caught up in owning the horse that you disrespect his space without an invitation. In fact, horses typically only lash out if they feel threatened and need to defend themselves. Don't put your horse in a position where he feels defensive. Through trust and respect you shouldn't need to deal with nasty behaviors but if you are reworking a horse with a past then you may need to assert yourself. Do it without vengeance and try to understand why the horse is acting that way.

We must try to understand other's histories and stories so that we don't need to be offended by their actions. Perhaps they are reacting to something from their past and not you. It is up to them to own that behavior and choose to keep it or change it. If you are clear, without violence, about what is and is not acceptable behavior, you can lead the horse to a new solution. It is important to stay consistent – don't ignore a behavior one day and lash out at it the next. It is also helpful to use positive reinforcement to encourage the behaviors you want. Some people worry that horses will become spoiled with too many rewards but, within boundaries, a well-timed reward for hard work and understanding will simply reinforce good behavior. Clear guidelines help the horse to feel more secure because he knows what is expected of him. Set your boundaries and then give the horse the freedom to make decisions within them. Through love and understanding you can both have boundaries yet remain connected.

It is time to stop imposing ourselves on the horse because, when we do, we close our hearts and damage our relationship. Exerting our control over the horse is an assumption that our opinion is right or that we are better than him. We need to let go of the thought "do as I say or else" which is so prominent in the barn. It is time to stop using horses as a feel good thing for human benefit. We need to be careful that even in the process of opening up to the idea of acting in a partnership and serving the horse that we do not still create unequal expectations. For example, just the other day I wanted to pet my dog so I called her to me. Though the act of petting is mutually beneficial, I am the one that wanted to initiate it so why would I expect her to wake up and cross the room? We need to level the playing field and have realistic expectations. The way we approach the horse will determine how the horse responds.

If training makes the horse feel good and empowered he will want to work with us. With clear guidance and boundaries the horse will choose to collaborate because he sees a benefit and it makes him feel secure. It will take some time to get to that point because his experience has taught him to expect a certain outcome from training. We have to show the horse that he is going to start gaining a benefit from training and that we are on a path to a meaningful, happy life together. We may initially be disappointed or frustrated that he does not want to. That is an opportunity for us to learn and to show him a new way. We do not get quality work from someone who does not want to do what we are asking. The movements we want from the horse require him to feel good and, if forced, will be sub-par. Not listening to the horse could even lead to pain or injury.

Riding and training is not a linear process where you accomplish something and never return to it. Even if we have had a horse for years it is never too late to go back to the basics to build skills, confidence, relationship, choice, and free will. Even a horse that is well trained and working on complicated moves will benefit from revisiting old concepts on occasion. In addition, riding doesn't always have to be hard work. Just because a horse can perform a sliding stop doesn't mean that we ask for one every time we want to halt. We have to maintain a balance in our training by combining basic skills with more complicated skills. Progress is rarely a steady march forward.

Going back to basics is about undoing something that we taught in the past and want to change for the future. Horses have long, solid memories that are essential to their prey animal nature to keep them safe. Sometimes we have to undo those memories, particularly if the horse is coming from a past where he was shut down or treated harshly. We need to make new memories. For example, if the horse was hit with a whip they will remember it and remain fearful. If we want to use the whip as a tool to communicate then we must first detach the fear reaction from the whip. For it to again become an effective tool he shouldn't even have "respect" for the whip – it must become a neutral extension of our hand. To build that trust we must find ways to slowly re-teach the horse.

If you get a new horse trained by someone else, start at the beginning and bring him forward on your own to ensure that he is physically and emotionally prepared for what you are asking. Training will obviously go faster with a horse that has already been trained but the process gives us a chance to build partnership, develop trust, and uncover any holes in their training. Just because a horse is jumping three foot courses doesn't mean that you have to start there. He may benefit from something as basic as working on leading exercises. In fact, leading the horse can help us create a connection. We can learn to actually lead the horse with respect and confidence rather than drag him around with a rope. Leading without a rope can be an opportunity to share our energy.

Other times going back to basics will involve deconstructing an issue before we can rebuild it. For example, if we have a horse that we want to compete in dressage but who is completely resistant to the bit due to a harsh handed rider in the past, we need to undo his fear and resistance. We can become creative by using a bit-less bridle to gain his trust. We need a bit to compete so we can eventually add cheek pieces to hold a bit in his mouth while we continue to ride off the bit-less bridle. Then we can add a second set of reins and slowly transition from bit-less to contact on the bit. This sort of retraining work is about staying within the horse's comfort zone to remain respectful and build trust. The second we rush the process and cross a boundary we slide back in the progress and lose some of the trust we are working so hard to gain.

Ultimately, the best teacher when learning how to create a new approach to riding and training is the horse himself. See training through his eyes to understand the ways in which it can be frightening. Ask him what the best approach to learning is for him. Listen to the horse's needs and develop a program that allows him to blossom. Each horse is unique and requires a different approach. Whether we are training a trail horse or a grand prix dressage horse, we must respect them for who they are. Don't think about what the horse can do for you and how to make him do it – that will turn him into a machine. Rather, we must ask how we can help the horse be brave, confident, and proud. Help the horse understand that we are there to take care of him and keep him safe.

This requires overcoming our own demons – the fear, anxiety, negative thoughts, and predator attitude.

Fostering partnership through play

Goals and linear thinking are the way of the human, the predator, who needs to think ahead to hunt. The horse thinks in a much more global, unfocused way. Owing to their prey animal nature, horses must maintain an awareness to detect threats. It is unrealistic to expect horses to be logical, think in linear terms, always cooperate, and never have an opinion or get nervous. They are not a car that can be turned on and off – they are sentient beings. Approach the horse without an agenda. We do not need to get him to do or be anything. Don't use equipment to mold the experience – just be authentic with a desire to play and allow the horse to come out of his shell and be who he is. Let the process unfold without a list of expectations and tasks to accomplish.

Your intention should be to create a mutually beneficial partnership based on valuing each other and supporting one another to make decisions that enhance the partnership. You don't have to work out all the details to start working toward your vision. Follow your inner wisdom in each moment and you will get there. Be grateful for that faith and just do the piece that is in front of you in the moment. Although it seems counter intuitive to think that you will achieve your desired results and goals by letting go of them, have a clear vision of your destination, let go of the details, and trust that the path will be revealed. Beware of falling into the need to teach your horse a lesson – that is ego wanting to be in charge. As soon as you assert yourself to prove you are in control, you have lost control. It is also easy to grow impatient, give up, and resort to old methods but it is worth the wait and the effort to work through the process.

Take your horse into an arena or round pen and let him loose. It is best to start at liberty with no ropes, halters, bits, or saddles. Your only plan should be to stay grounded without an intention of getting him to do anything with you other than to connect. Focused work will come later. If he runs and bucks, run and play with him. If he just stands there, hang out with him. Don't ask for anything. Just follow his lead and encourage him to pay attention to you. As soon as he starts tuning into you and connecting, call it a day. Once your horse realizes that you don't have an agenda he will become more focused on you and curious. The horse can teach you to listen, play, and relax. Try committing to a task outside of the typical training realm, such as playing with a ball. Remain detached from an outcome and see if you can start to communicate your desires through your energy.

Work with your horse's natural instincts and characteristics. Horses are unbelievably curious and most of them love to play. They learn by playing with one another and are typically willing to give us a chance if we are authentic in our desire to play. Use that drive to make your work together fun, interesting, and novel. Use obstacle courses, poles, cones, barrels, props, balls, tarps, platforms, and anything else you have on hand to help build his confidence, have fun, and learn. Encourage his curiosity and let him explore rather than inventing inflexible rules about how to play. Take your horse on adventures to step over logs, investigate funny looking objects, or splash in a creek. You can use hills, raised poles, and different footing to create novelty, build muscle, and encourage the horse to use his full range of motion. Let him free jump or play with cattle, even if that is not part of your discipline.

Get creative and let you inner child out for a romp. Laugh, have fun, enjoy the experience – training doesn't have to be serious all the time. Think of how wonderful it is to play with a dog or cat, for both the animal and the person. For some reason we don't approach horses the same way but it's called 'horse play' for a reason. So go horse around. Relax and don't take the horse so seriously. We want to be around horses, so let it be fun, experiment, and don't be afraid to break the rules.

Playing with the horse on their terms is powerful for the horse. It gives them a chance to unravel past experiences with training and human interaction. It gives them a chance to forgive the transgressions of humans. It is also a way for them to learn new ways to move and relate to the world that are fun and empowering. Meanwhile, we have a chance to undo old thought patterns and the rigid determination to get the horse to cooperate. Through play you can begin to build trust and respect for one another.

When we do ground work with horses we typically stand in the middle and drive the horse around us with the help of a rope or walls to prevent the horse from leaving. Instead, give the horse a large space, freedom of his head, and the choice to participate. This will take more time than the traditional way but it will also be more rewarding. Though we could chase a horse around a round pen and get him to submit to us in a short time, doing so doesn't mean we have earned his trust. This is why it is so important to take the time to interact in new ways and create a new connection that serves everyone.

A round pen can be a good way to connect as well – there is no "right" way to build partnership and trust. Try travelling with the horse side by side and playing and interacting in a way that he understands. It is also okay to let the horse move your feet on occasion as long as he is not aggressive or bullying you. Take turns leading the play like a dialogue back and forth. Allow him to initiate new ideas.

We can also break out of the box of always working one on one with horses. Horses don't live in pairs and partner up the way humans do. They function in dynamic herds so we have a lot to learn from that setting. Work with multiple horses or an entire herd. You will learn more about them and yourself. This is not for training – it is for exploration. Observe their behaviors as they interact and play together. Join them in play. How do you affect the dynamics? Horses will feel safer when surrounded by others and new facets of your horse's personality may surface. You also get the chance to become part of an authentic community and may find a place of belonging in a different society. This is all about interacting with the horse as a horse.

Whatever shape this work takes, keep it fun. We always ask horses to live in our world, play our games, and follow our rules. This is a chance to respect the horse and see things through his perspective. It is a joyful experience when your horse starts playing with you out of desire rather than subjugation. The time spent playing goes a long way to developing a partnership that promotes a willing attitude. Don't keep score – it's not that kind of game. Give yourself and the horse the freedom to make mistakes, try something different, or choose another way. If the horse learns that expressing himself or making a choice that differs from yours leads to a correction he will become less likely to try for you which will carry over into all of your training.

A change of dynamics: from ground work to riding

Ground work is critical to building partnerships and should be maintained throughout the horse's life. Eventually we start riding and stop doing as much on the ground but our relationship changes when we shift from the ground to their backs. Time out of the saddle is critical to learn, play, and communicate for horse and human. The ground can be a safer place to learn and any mistakes by either party will have less impact. There are different implications if your horse chooses to buck, spook, or not listen when you are riding. Once a solid base has been built on the ground you can naturally turn to riding with a holistic approach of love, respect, and understanding.

We do not have an inherent right to climb on to the horse's back. He must consent and invite you. We no longer tell the horse that he should let us ride him and, instead, show him how to carry us and why that is beneficial to him. On his back we can shift from separateness to oneness. When it is time to get on a horse for the first time do not focus on how to make the horse let you get on him. Instead, ask yourself how you can develop the confidence, cooperation, and partnership that naturally lead you to riding. Getting on the horse for the first time can be a non-issue for both of you. Yes, riding is enjoyable for you, but it is time to ensure it is so for all parties involved.

Horses who work in an empowered way will come to appreciate you on their back. Sitting on the horse is a place of trust for both parties. There should be no fear on the part of the horse or human when you get on his back. If you have built partnership on the ground, the horse should trust you to sit on him and you should trust the horse to carry you. When on his back you are in constant contact with one another. This means that you can take your partnership to the next level and support each other further. You can travel together. You can communicate on both sides of the horse rather than just one side when on the ground. From here you can explore new surroundings, movement, thoughts, ideas, and feelings.

Sitting on the back of a horse is a very sacred space of honor. Often we forget just what a feat this act is – two very different animals coming together to ride and be ridden. For both the horse and rider this is a huge act of faith and trust in the other. For the horse to accept and willingly carry a predator on his back is one of the greatest examples of the horse's kind and forgiving heart. We sit in a space where a mountain lion might grab hold to take the horse down. It is one of the most unnatural things that we could ask a horse to do and yet he has willingly carried mankind through history.

While sitting perched atop a horse fills us with awe and wonderment, it is a different story for the horse. On his back we are sitting in his blind spot. He can no longer see us. This means that he must learn to communicate through an entirely different system than ever before. Horses do not embrace. The only time horses spend touching for prolonged periods of time is during grooming sessions or while breeding. They are very adept at reading energy but most of their communication and perception is based on reading visual cues. Without the ability to make visual contact with us, the horse must learn to feel what we want. The horse always senses energy but this is a physical feel which is totally foreign. Much of the ground work you did to prepare for this was through body language and that ceases once in the saddle creating a very large learning curve for the horse. Once we are in the saddle we often do not give the horse a full translation dictionary from the language of "see" to "feel".

In addition, they must learn a whole new way of moving and carrying their body with the added weight of the rider. We sit just behind the shoulders on the portion of the back that has the least support. The horse's spine articulates with the pelvis in the hind end and then is suspended by muscles and ligaments all the way up to the head. The entire weight of the body, and now your weight as well, is held up in a muscular sling between the front legs. Think about the added strain that must cause the horse. Think about the added concussion in his limbs. So he must compensate by finding a new center of gravity and changing his movement to accommodate us.

On their backs we are more vulnerable and that can lead us to start controlling the horse again. On the ground at liberty it is easier to allow them to act up or ignore us. Once we start riding it is easy to become defensive because we feel insecure. If the horse does something desirable we pat ourselves on the back, but if he does something less than desirable we blame the horse. We need to understand that horses act out by rearing or bucking as a reaction to confusion, fear, or pain. You do not have to punish them if you can illuminate the underlying problem. Spooking, on the other hand, is your horse being a horse. You can't get upset about it if you want to encourage the horse to turn to you for help. If, when in crisis, you get fearful or angry you are proving you aren't a reliable, trustworthy leader.

Don't look at the horse as being disobedient. They have their own needs and wants. When they choose to do something different than what you had in mind look at it as constructive criticism. Ask yourself what you need to change. What can you change internally to achieve the desired outcome or to accept a different result? It can be viewed as a learning opportunity for both of you rather than a disobedience to be punished. When you learn to listen you can make changes to become more authentic and the horse will in turn become a more willing, enthusiastic partner. Every time your horse does something good or naughty it is a gift and a glimpse into yourself, your partnership, and authentic interaction. Is there a way to let go of trying to change the horse and instead look for ways to change you? The horse isn't vindictive and he is just reacting to what is.

If you become defensive, or fearful, it is easy to become angry, lash out, and demand compliance. As soon as you blow up, stomp toward your horse, and look at him with sharp eyes it is only natural for your horse to think he is about to become dinner. You simply can't slip into this predatory response if you want to prevent the horse from turning into a prey animal who can only focus on staying safe rather than learning. What do you gain if you get frustrated and lash out? Is that actually beneficial to solving the issue? Does it help you work toward partnership or does it harm your relationship? How does this show up in other relationships in your life? Your attitude is a choice and the need for more, to be right, or to win is ego talking. Your heart would rather stay in a state of cooperation instead of competition. You can learn to take the path of least resistance.

It is easy to become frightened on a horse that is spooky or unpredictable. We can build our confidence on their back by helping the horse to feel more confident in his environment to reduce his reactivity to stimuli. Horses are, by nature, easily frightened and we have put them in a situation that takes away their ability to listen to their instinct to run away. It is our responsibility to educate the horse emotionally as well as physically.

Building confidence in the horse

We must teach the horse how to be successful in our world by teaching each new concept in a non-threatening way and slowly building on it within the tolerance range of the horse. Show your horse that you can make him feel better, more secure, and less anxious. It is to his advantage to work with someone who is not another flight animal. You can help ground him and mitigate his fear. You can be his rock to help turn his fear and flight into curiosity and play. In turn you will gain more confidence as you start to trust that the horse isn't going to do something that inadvertently causes you harm.

One method to help build confidence in your partnership is to ensure that the horse has the skills to thrive in our human environment. The horse needs to know that no harm is going to come to him. That means always working without fear or pain. Start by touching him often with love and compassion. For the horse to accept training he must first accept you. He should have no fear of you. Touching him everywhere and getting him to the point that he finds it enjoyable is essential to him accepting your touch and feel on his back. Show him that any equipment you use, such as a whip or ropes, are just an extension of your hand. Touch him everywhere with these items so there is no fear of your equipment. To prove that it is not there to hurt him you must never use the equipment in an abusive manner. Then use different items like a towel, saddle pad, plastic bag, or feather duster to teach him that we are not going to cause him harm even if an item seems frightening at first.

Practice bathing, blanketing, fly spraying, clipping, tacking up, or taking your jacket off while on him. A horse who does not react to strange things in his environment is safe to work around. Remember that this is a process and the horse could react strongly to certain things you introduce. Don't let him spook you or move you around physically or emotionally. You must work on your confidence as well to be a confident leader through this process. If the horse explodes you will likely remove the stimulus that scared him, allowing the horse to calm down. He will then start training you to back off when he is upset so that he gets what he wants. Be aware of his ability to train you so that you back off only after he has calmed down. You are in control. Practice advance and retreat where you introduce an item and wait for the horse to relax, soften, or give a decent try. Then you can remove the item as a reward for his effort. He is free to have his meltdown without rebuke but it is quietness that earns a reward.

To build trust we must show the horse that he is safe in our presence. He needs to learn to turn to you for guidance and safety. You want him to see your time together as a fun opportunity to play, learn, and feel good about himself. You can become the reward because you provide comfort. Teach him that being around you is positive so that he comes to want to be with you. Get creative with bouncy balls, bikes, umbrellas, flags, funny hats, or noisy things. A spook-free horse is a gem so teach him to accept all sorts of stimuli and look to you for confidence. Be sure not to over-face him, which will have the opposite effect. If you ask for too much you risk the horse shutting down or permanently losing his trust in you. Take your time, keep it safe, and have fun.

Horses are curious by nature but also very cautious. They will explore and examine strange things in their environment by using an approach and retreat method. They look at it from different angles and take their time approaching it. As humans we want to take a direct approach and push the horse to do the same. We could solve a lot of spookiness with a little patience. Give the horse the freedom of his head and let him figure it out. Do not demand that the horse investigate something: rather ask him to investigate and encourage him with your own courage. Encourage the curiosity, respect the cautious, and minimize the spook.

Each horse is an individual. They all react differently to situations, struggle with different concepts, and enjoy different things. You must look at your horse as unique. Some horses think it's fun to try new things and others don't. Highly sensitive horses may have trouble with bomb-proofing exercises or being ridden. With those horses you have to move slowly and ask for permission with every step, every day, or they could become explosive, irritated, or disassociated. All horses benefit from being desensitized, within their comfort zone, to things they need to accept but be careful not to train their sensitivity out of them entirely. We want horses to be brave and safe to work around but we also want them to hear and respond to the slightest cues and aids from us rather than ignore them as static noise. Don't shut the horse down but help him live in the human world. It's a fine line.

Don't try to fix your horse or shut down his feelings. Be a supportive presence on his path to authentic power. Allow him to live his truth. Do not try to shut down the horse's fear or chastise him for spooking at "nothing". Honor his truth and help him get to the root of the feeling. Let him experience his truth and power without labeling it as good or bad. Your judgment of others does nothing to help them overcome an issue or thrive in their authenticity. Be empathetic and hold the space for him to express himself. This is hard to do and requires you to let go of the belief that you know what is best or what is right and wrong.

Just like you can't teach yourself to never have a certain emotion, you can't teach the horse to never feel frightened or frisky. Through training, awareness, and practice you can teach the horse to allow the emotion to happen, acknowledge it, and make a choice of how to respond. We want the horse to use the same emotional awareness that we are learning. The horse may spook but through trust in you and the practice of investigation, he can make a choice to not run, buck, or bolt. Courage is a product of practice. You cannot will yourself or the horse to become courageous in the face of fear. We must all practice facing our fears without getting hurt and we become better at it over time and eventually more courageous. The fear doesn't go away but we have the skill to deal with it. You can certainly never overcome fear with force; force will cause resistance or avoidance. We must embrace the fear to overcome it.

If you have a youngster, training him to accept stimuli is essential to the learning process. Even if you acquired a fully trained horse go ahead and assume this was never done and do it. If he has been trained in this manner it will become apparent but if he hasn't you can give your horse much more confidence and make your life together easier and your work together safer. Don't get stuck in the common training concepts of your discipline. I see more people in western and trail riding communities use this wisdom but it is a much more rare sight in a hunter/jumper or elite dressage barn. Why is that? It benefits all horses. How awesome would it be if your jumper was unfazed by the sight of flapping flags or tarps on the ground?

Building confidence in the horse is not so that he will no longer work for you. It is so that he will choose to work with you because he sees a benefit to the work. Everyone wants to feel good. Everyone is content as a result of doing something joyful. As the horse grows to trust you he will take bigger risks. If we cultivate that, the horse will start to offer to work with you more. Willingness and trust, which are built on the ground, create a safe ride. Every rider will get into trouble at some point but if you have a confident horse and trust between you as a team you should be able to work your way out of most situations in a safe manner. Trust the process and the magic of a synergistic partnership.

We must learn to trust ourselves and build confidence before we can trust our partner. When you develop confidence in yourself you can lift others up rather than pushing others down in an effort to make you feel better. You must work with the horse to establish the respect and trust essential to a partnership. Without confidence we judge ourselves, feel judged by others, compare ourselves to others, and try to dominate and control others. Lack of confidence leaves us ruled by our emotions, living in fear, lost in the world, and living a life of limited potential. With confidence we develop power and no longer need to talk negatively about others or ourselves. We can honor others' opinion and strengths and instill confidence in them. With confidence we are present, aware of our emotions, and can live on point in a big way.

Horses are inspired by a confident person who lives on purpose and follows through on their path. Confidence in the horse is built through allowing the horse to act authentically. If you stifle his character he can never find his courage. Confidence is not gained from outer things nor is it about becoming arrogant. It is an acknowledgement of yourself, an inner knowing. This belief and trust in yourself is strengthened by your dedication to living your truth in service to others. It is knowing that you can manifest your dreams and become a realized human being. Having confidence is not about having all the answers or even being competent; it is about believing in your dreams, following through with them, taking care of yourself, and creating boundaries based on what best serves your soul. Developing these skills in the arena allows you to carry them into the rest of your life.

Chapter Four:
Intuitive Awareness

***Intuition:** the power or faculty of knowing things without conscious reasoning*
***Awareness:** the state of having perception or knowledge*

Our emotions make up an energetic guiding system that sends us messages from our higher self. In our society, we are taught to suppress negative emotion and strive for positive emotion. When we do not listen to every message from our soul we are denying our internal GPS. Learn to listen to what your mind and body are telling you about your emotional state so that you can move into your heart and act in the moment according to the desires of your soul. Discover the stillness that surrounds your thoughts and feelings to become less reactive and more empowered. The only way to fully unleash your power and live a life of unlimited potential is by developing emotional awareness and listening to your intuition.

Intuitive awareness is about feeling your emotions in the moment and allowing them to flow through you with non-attachment. To empower your heart you can't bury your emotions – they need to be heard and honored. You can't deny yourself of who you are. That means letting go of the person you were so you can become the person you are capable of being. Staying present means facing unpleasant or painful feelings without turning away. When you turn away you are avoiding your truth and it keeps you from being able to heal and come into your own.

Embracing emotion

Fear, self-doubt, self-hatred, jealousy, envy, anger, despair, greed, hate, criticism, etc. all put limitations on you and your power. You need to become aware of how those feelings affect you in order to nurture the self-love and compassion that will set you free. Everyone has good and bad within them which makes everyone perfect in their own way. Emotional freedom is not about getting rid of your emotions or only having good feelings. If you move into your emotions they can inform you and flow through you to help you heal and find your inner power, strength, wisdom, and intuition. Don't judge your emotions because all emotions provide universal guidance. Whether good or bad, emotions are not permanent. Acceptance of the transient nature of emotions allows for liberation in the present.

Though emotions make us feel good or bad, emotions themselves are not inherently good or bad. They are just providing you with energetic information. Whether you feel confident, anxious, joyful, sad, peaceful, or angry, you are receiving temporary messages on a sliding scale that can help you determine how to act. We want to encourage the frequency and intensity of the emotions we enjoy but those too are just what they are in the moment and will fade again. They are like waves that come and go. We become trapped when we strive to control the duration of feelings. No emotion is lasting. We can only encourage the good feelings to happen more often and feel more powerful while diminishing the frequency and intensity of the bad feelings. Just as a battery requires a positive and negative charge, we require energy from the entire spectrum to inform us.

Do not deny any emotion. There are feelings that we believe we should feel and we only want to embrace those, but then you are ignoring the wisdom of your inner self. Embrace all emotions with a clear mind to discover the message they hold. All emotions have the power to heal if you listen and take action – it is your choice. Strong positive emotions can be just as overwhelming as strong negative ones. Breathe into the sensations in your body, feel the ground under your feet, and connect with the energy within you. Ask yourself what is real about the emotion. What is it actually saying – not what you want it to say but the truth it holds? Often the hard part is accepting and acting on the response that you receive.

You cannot create a life of fulfillment, joy, and meaning if you continually block your emotions or are unaware of how you feel. You have to work through the pain, the doubt, and the fear to be able to release it. Avoiding those things doesn't mean they are not there. Avoidance simply means that you are allowing them to persist and grow in intensity. When we ignore the message, the soul finds more ways to be heard. People often have patterns of emotions in their lives. Throughout life you continually come across situations that make you feel a certain way. The circumstances change but the feeling is the same. It is as though the emotion is stuck in your body and you just keep reliving it. This is an indication that you need to change some belief about yourself or the world.

In order to utilize your emotions as your internal guidance system you have to learn to quiet the mind and change your beliefs. You have to let go of the stories, obsessions, and addictions to thoughts and things in order to get out of your head and into your heart. We often become addicted to repetitive, negative thought patterns even though they make us feel bad because it is what we know – it feels familiar and comfortable. You have to make a decision to become aware of those patterns and turn off the recording in your head.

Mind, body, and heart

Your mind is the only thing that can lie, travel to the past or future, or make decisions. It is a powerful tool but, if you don't know how to use it the mind can get you into trouble. The mind allows us to judge our emotions and label them as good or bad. Based on that label we either grasp for more of the feeling or reject the feeling. The mind is a tool to connect your body and your soul. Thought gives us the power of choice and the ability to reason. We can decide if we want to listen to our emotions and how to act on them. We develop our persona, memories, and dreams through thoughts however, the mind is not all that you truly are, even though your ego would like to say that it is.

Everything is relative and our perceptions of the world are based on our beliefs and experiences, creating and forming the reality we live. It is hard to break through the negative discourse in our minds but as long as we are stuck in this way of thinking we will view ourselves and others through a negative filter. The mind and the ego want to label everything to know what it is. If we can let go of the labels we can change our beliefs, perceptions, and self-image. The power to change comes with first accepting what is and realizing that there are no mistakes in our lives, just false labels and mental misperceptions.

The mind can be used to interpret negative emotions and feelings either as a message to help you improve your life or to feed you more negative emotions. Your mind can be used for good or allowed to spiral out of control causing destruction. Our society, language, and education train the mind to attach to the physical self. Beauty, success, wealth, knowledge, skills, and fame all develop the ego, the persona. If we break out of that cage and limit the importance of the physical self, we can become less attached to all of the external things that we think we need to be happy. It is the ego that constantly thinks that achieving certain milestones or acquiring a critical mass of possessions will result in our happiness but these ideas are inaccurate, ego-driven, social constructs.

Progress is impossible without change and the only thing that you can change for certain is your mind. Change your mind and change the world. This isn't easy to do and can take a lifetime to master but every effort is a step closer to a blissful life. Tend to your mind like a veggie patch. Negative thoughts are like weeds growing out of control and some of them have very deep roots so they keep coming back. You must dig down and get to the root of an issue before you can get rid of a belief for good. Meanwhile, you plant the seeds of positive thoughts. It is not enough to just plant them; you must lovingly tend to them to help them grow. You nourish and water them. It takes some time but eventually you get the fruits of your labor – nourishing thoughts that feed and sustain you. Overtime you have a prolific garden full of beautiful expressions. You never stop weeding, as negative thoughts will always pop up, but there are more veggies than anything.

Positive thinking can be a very powerful tool but only when you are authentic about it. If it is phony, without emotion, or you don't believe in what you are thinking, then it is useless. If you are still turbulent on the inside, your effort to override the negative thoughts is powerless. You will only be effective with positive thinking as long as you are aware of your inner world and not trying to force good things to happen. More important than generating positive thoughts that get lost in the chaos in your mind is to stop the incessant chatter in your head. Freedom, peace, love, and joy come from working through the voice of your ego and living from a different place. Quieting the mind helps you peel back all of your identities so that you are left with your true self.

As you work on changing your inner landscape you will still feel anger, sadness, or fear, but those feelings become sign posts pointing you in the right direction rather than controlling you.

Your anger helps you to fight against injustice, the sadness lets you know when something is missing, and the fear gives you a moment to pause and reflect on your decision. You can start to use your emotions to help guide you, to be in tune with your instincts and intuition, and to let you experience the fullness of life.

Can you become aware of your negative qualities and reframe them in a positive light? Can you turn your judgment into decisiveness, jealousy into wanting the best for yourself, greed into embracing abundance, or obsession into focus? We are all unique in our combination of good and bad qualities and they make us who we are. Embrace your true nature and find ways to utilize your talents. Build on your good qualities and bring your passion into existence. Not only do you deserve it but so does everyone else. If you withhold your light the whole world is darker.

Body awareness is also essential for developing emotional awareness. You don't think anxious – you feel anxious in your body and you worry in your mind. One is a thought process and the other is a feeling. They are linked together in the body. How do you know what you are feeling emotionally? You feel it in your body. If you are anxious then you may have a knot in your stomach that tells your brain to translate your emotion as anxiety. Therefore you have to be in touch with your body to know what you are feeling. You also need to be able stop the cycle of worrying in your head to move into the feeling and receive its message without feeding it with your ego's beliefs.

The body is the physical manifestation that houses our mind, ego, heart, soul, emotions, and spirit. The body can receive information from physical, mental, or spiritual stimuli. The brain is responsible for processing all that information but it can't do that if it is not trained to listen to the physical and spiritual feedback. Gaining awareness allows you to create a filter for what you take in and what you put out. It gives you a barometer for your spiritual and physical well-being. Our emotions move through the body changing our behavior and our actions. They also affect every cell in your body by changing the chemicals and energy throughout your system. This is why negative emotion can eventually lead to disease and why changing your thoughts can help to heal your body.

Your thoughts become emotions and your emotions show up in your body. If you have a joyful perspective you will feel happy and your body will respond with all of the chemicals, energy, and movements that exude happiness. You need to become aware of how your emotions show up in your body. The way your body communicates with you isn't necessarily the same as everyone else. For example, fear shows up for me as a burning, empty sensation in my solar plexus or stomach region. For years I thought I was hungry when in reality I was just feeding my apprehension. For other people that fear could be in your heart or your throat. Listen to what your body is telling you.

Emotions are not caused by other people or circumstances – they are a result of your reactions to those people and circumstances. It all boils down to love and fear. Positive and negative reactions stem from love and fear respectively. Everything is energy. Our feelings and thoughts are all prayers that we are sending out and the universe will respond so that we receive more of the same. Tune yourself into the things you want and the universe has no choice but to respond. We can choose to be happy regardless of our external circumstances by listening to our emotions, unlocking creativity, and finding purpose. The mind can translate that into action and expression in your physical body.

We can learn to live in service to our true self – the soul. The mind can connect your personality and physical body through your emotions, opening the ability for you to be in service to the true desires and expression of your spiritual self. When the mind comes to value your inner being and work in service to it, you can find fulfillment. As long as the mind is in service to the ego or external things it will continue looking out there for fulfillment while denying painful emotions. Those emotions are energetic messages from your heart and soul telling you that you are not on the right track. Physical solutions, such as making more money, do not speak to the soul. Your physical needs will be met with a quiet mind in service to a fulfilled soul. You will develop reverence for your body which is a vessel to carry who you truly are.

Finding your authentic self and becoming in touch with your emotions is a bit like peeling away the layers of an onion. It often stings temporarily, makes you cry at times, and there are different sized layers that vary in their difficulty to remove, but eventually you reach the center. It's not always easy but each time you work with your horse is an opportunity to work on the next layer to get a little deeper on your journey to the center. It takes time, insight, and courage but it is worth the journey. Getting in touch with your emotions and not letting them control you is the path to authentic power. With inner power you crave harmony, cooperation, sharing, and collaboration. You no longer need to grasp for external power that exerts control over others or your circumstance. You can develop a love of life, accept what is, and go with the flow. We all want a life without unnecessary pain.

Our thoughts and emotions work together to weave our reality. You think about something and the way you think about it, based on your beliefs and perception, causes an emotion to well up within you. That energy is then emitted and emoted into the world and more things with that energy are attracted to it, and you, like a magnet. What are you putting out? Is that really what you want to receive? Learning to control the mind and our energy has direct implications on the quality of life we lead. Horses give us the space to practice this and receive direct and immediate feedback to learn how to use our emotions and energy to create our reality, choose how to react to external circumstances, and find inner stillness and joy.

Working with the horse to deepen your emotional awareness

The horse is tuned into your authentic self, your soul, rather than your false self, your ego. The horse cannot understand the stories of your persona and reacts to who you really are and what you're feeling. The horse creates a safe space and a sounding board for all of your deepest thoughts and he will keep your secrets because he does not understand them. At a deeper level he can not only let you vent without judgment, he can read your energy. Horses are much more sensitive and adept at reading body language and energy fields. They are physically cautious but emotionally courageous. They are masters of emotion and can help you translate and see what you are putting out into the world. We are all concentrated bubbles of energy living in an energy field. Embracing that can change the way you work with horses so that you can connect from the heart, work with and channel energy, and allow the horse to care for you at times.

When we are not aware, are denying our emotions, or are out of touch with our body we become incongruent. Perhaps your physical, bodily experience is not aligned with your beliefs or your emotions. Or perhaps the words in your head and the stories you tell yourself are in conflict with how you feel. When you become congruent and authentic you create an energetic wholeness with an aligned body, mind, and soul. This is important when working with horses because they are unbalanced by individuals who are not authentic and congruent. They do not understand why your actions do not match your energy and can become agitated, distrusting, or choose to not connect with you.

The ability of horses to read our emotions is a gift for us, if we use it properly. They can help us to come into alignment so that we can make the inner changes necessary to living a happy life. You can have bad days, as we all do, but be honest with yourself and your horse. You can't take it out on the horse nor can you hide it from him. We are so determined in our culture to hide our feelings but, no matter how nice your mask is, the horse will see through it. Often times other humans see through it as well. Sometimes you can just sense that there is something false about a person and no one wants to trust or be led by someone who is hiding something or dishonest. So work through it with mindfulness, admitting to yourself how you feel, and embracing those feelings. You also have to recognize and respect that horses also have bad days. So if you can't work together positively then back off and don't push it.

You don't have to get rid of your emotions for the horse to respond in a positive manner. Instead, you must own and acknowledge the emotions so that you are congruent. Allow your body and emotions to speak without repressing it. Learn to listen and relate to your horse through energy. What sensations do you feel? Just as your horse doesn't lie, neither does your body or feelings. When you feel pain physically or emotionally, ask yourself what you need to know. What is the pain trying to tell you? Listen to your inner voice and inner power. Everyone has will power but only some are willing to listen and change. Your soul doesn't lie and will always lead you in a direction that will serve you.

You do not have control over external situations until you change internal labels and thoughts. The things that show up in your life over and over again will often present themselves as a learning opportunity when you are working with horses. Perhaps you feel that you are always rejected, pushed around, a failure, or that others do wrong by you – and you will see those things in your interactions with the horse.

If you always feel rejected then it may seem as though the horse doesn't want to work with you, walks away, or is impervious to your attempts to motivate him. Until you believe that you are worthy and deserving, this scenario will continue to repeat. If you always feel pushed around, maybe you will have a horse who literally pushes and shoves you or doesn't respect your space – until you respect yourself, find your power, and establish boundaries. If you feel like you are a failure, maybe you will see your horse's actions as a failure and as though you can't ever do anything right – until you believe you are capable and deserving of success. If you feel that others always do wrong by you, you may read the horse's actions as acting out toward you and as though the horse is constantly disobeying – until you face the anger, stop judging, and let other's stuff be their stuff.

The horse gives you a space to learn how to change your inner world and the dialogue in your head to break the cycle of circumstances that continually appear in your life. Would you prefer to live with fear- and doubt-based thinking or love- and trust-based thinking? Your emotions are like your energy sensor. What are you putting out? Is it positive or negative? How does the situation make you feel? Why is that the feeling you're receiving? Do you want to cultivate more of that or change it?

Let go of preconceived ideas and labels. If you think something will be hard or scary it will be. Furthermore, your horse can pick up on your negativity. Your horse can reflect your emotions and thoughts back to you because he can read the changes in your body. If you doubt that your horse will do something your intent and body language will convey that to the horse, creating a self-fulfilling prophecy and affirming your doubt. You have to let go and banish self-doubt and negative thoughts. If your beliefs shape your reality, then why not paint a beautiful, positive life with your thoughts?

When practicing this technique, it is of the utmost importance to believe in the fundamental concept that putting out positivity will return positivity. If you doubt the concept is true or that it will work, you will filter your experiences through that underlying disbelief and affirm that it doesn't work. However, if you can take a leap of faith, the horses can show you the power of your mind so that you can see immediate results. Then you can make it part of your belief system and internal dialogue and you can carry this skill into all areas of your life.

Mindful awareness

A lot of spiritual practices point to mindfulness as the key to unlocking happiness. When a horse is interacting with you, he is present. The human, on the other hand, is often worrying about the argument she had with her spouse that morning or the big presentation she is going to give at work later in the week. There is often an incessant dialogue in the mind that prevents us from living in a state of awareness. Do you ever get so caught up in your thoughts as you're driving down the road that you suddenly realize you don't remember the last 10 miles? You miss out on life when the chatter in your mind takes over.

As soon as you take your attention away from the horse and start thinking about other things you are no longer focused on the horse. If you aren't focused on the horse, there is no reason to be working with him. When you are not present you are missing your life. When you check out into daydreams of the future or old movies of the past you are not fully living and experiencing. We use our past experiences to inform us and our goals for the future to guide us, but you can only live and make decisions now. When you are not in this moment, you are essentially surrendering your power and stating that your life, right now, isn't worth living. You are too busy thinking about things that do not exist. Your life is a short, precious gift. Every moment counts because once it passes you can't get it back. Don't waste it.

Meditation is a great tool to connect to your inner self and accept what is. Meditation leads you to develop self-knowledge and clarity. Gaining control of your mind allows you to find health, success, joy, and a connection with your horse. You can use meditation before you work with the horse, or in his presence, to move out of the ego and into your heart so that you can connect from your heart, be aware of your horse and your body, and become grounded into the earth. Meditation helps bring you into the moment and quiets the mind so that you can become aware of your body and your emotions. We tend to live in a fish bowl, completely unaware of what is happening below the neck. Horses rely on us to interact with them outside of the mind, so finding ways to do that will improve all of your work with them.

Meditation is a way to awaken your senses so that you can feel, tune into your body, and move into your emotions. It is not a system to bypass everything and close yourself off by shutting down the mind. You cannot spiritually bypass the enormity and complexity of who you really are – mind, body, and soul. It is simply a way to balance the playing field so that the ego isn't always in control. Positive thinking and quieting the mind doesn't mean that bad things will never happen to you. It just gives you the space to make a choice to feel your emotions rather than label the situation so that you can act according to your authentic self rather than your ego. It also allows for you to find balance in your body and your life.

One of the most difficult, and important, things to develop in riding is a sense of feel and timing. Instructors and trainers can give you guidance but it's a bit like laughing. You can't know the feeling of laughter unless you have done it. You can describe aspects of what it feels like but it must be experienced for you to truly understand. The same is true when you are seeking the perfect feeling of balance and harmony in the moment with your horse. It remains somewhat mysterious and elusive until you have experienced it. The horse can lead you to that feel through awareness better than any human can, but it requires you to be completely aware of yourself and the horse. One way to achieve that is by using riding as a moving meditation to feel how the rhythm of the horse ripples through your body and how movement in your body affects his stride. There is a beautiful symbiosis when you get it right.

You can do this on your own but it is even more helpful to have someone lunge the horse for you so that you can become fully aware without having to worry about your surroundings or steering. This is a great way to get out of your head and find your balance. Even better is to ride bareback so that the feel of your horse under you is amplified and you can melt into one without equipment in the way. I also love to ride to music and allow that to influence my creativity and start to dance with the horse. These techniques really allow you to become aware of your body and discover your center. Move into the sensations in your body to feel for tension or imbalances. In riding your body mechanics, position, balance, and body language are all essential for success so it pays to tune in.

Finding balance with the horse will help you to find balance in your life on all levels but this is not a magical potion that will fix all of your problems without any effort. We treasure quick-fix solutions in our society with all of our fad diets, pills, and products that will change our health, fitness, or looks without having to do anything. We tend to look outside ourselves for someone else to tell us who we are, who we should be, or what we should do. The horse is not there to give us those answers. He can serve as support and as a mirror for you to be able to reflect your inner self to uncover the answers your soul already knows. We are not anthropomorphizing the horses or assigning our characteristics to them. We are empowering them so that they can react honestly to our energy, which is a reflection of who you are and how you are feeling.

Being fully aware in the present allows you to feel the initial stirrings of an emotion so that you can react to it before it grows into a monster and blind-sides you. When you ride with awareness you have the chance to say "hey, I'm getting a little frustrated," which allows you to make a change in that moment, that stride. Even if you can't change what is happening, you can change the way you choose to react to it. Conversely, you can also catch the moment when you realize "hey, this is perfect" so that you can cultivate that feeling, encourage the horse, and enjoy it while it's happening. It is only in this moment that you have the power to act and ability to feel what the horse is doing. It is through your thoughts and actions now that shape the unlimited possibilities of the future.

Challenging emotions

Each emotion is there for a reason and can teach you something. With self-inquiry you can find new solutions to problems. You can use your creativity to break down a miscommunication or misunderstanding and find a successful way to solve the problem without harming yourself or the horse. Give the horse a say in the solution. Allow him to provide insight. Let him teach you how to let go and feel joy. Exude love and kindness but stay in touch with all of the feelings that well up inside of you as you ride. It is often the negative feelings that we focus on and get us in trouble, and those often hold the biggest lessons because they illuminate areas that aren't working or that could use improvement. Everything happens for a reason so use it. Each emotion has a different lesson for each individual.

I see a lot of anger in equestrians that stems from fear and feeling powerless when trying to learn to work with such a large animal. Anger can come from the frustration of not being able to arrange your life and the things in it the way you want. When you feel fearful or like you aren't good enough or have enough then you lose your power. You may overcompensate by acting out in anger, trying to assert power that you really don't have. From this place you cause harm to others and the horse. You must heal the underlying cause of the anger. The ego and a lack of confidence can both lead to the need to be right and to defend yourself at all cost.

When you grow angry or frustrated with the horse or feel the need to punish him or show him who is boss, what are you really angry about? Why do you need to be the boss? What is the feeling that comes before the feeling that you can't ignore? Start to listen to the subtle signals so that your emotions don't need to escalate. If your horse refuses a jump in the show ring your reaction may be to kick him or hit him over the fence. What does that do for your partnership? Is that your pride talking? Is it your horse's fault? Are your nerves contributing to the refusal? Did you fully prepare him for the task at hand? It's okay to be assertive but not at the expense of others.

Don't hold onto your frustration or it will get stuck in the body and cause disease. You need to give it a voice, rather than suppress it, but you need to find a healthy outlet for it instead of acting out toward the horse or other loved ones. Frustration can be a good thing. It shows you when something needs to change. Too often we slip into the "I can't" way of thinking. Instead figure out what you can do to make it work. It is hard to shed things in your life, but necessary. Allow yourself to cry and grieve if you need to. "Real men don't cry" is a bunch of garbage. Crying is one of your natural ways to release emotions from your body, whether caused by frustration, sadness, or joy. You must let it flow, literally, to cleanse you or all of that squelched emotion will ferment in your body and make you sick emotionally, mentally, and physically.

Stress comes from a loss of control, an uncertainty, or an internal pressure from not being in alignment. What would it feel like to have a stress free day or have, for both of you, a stress free training session? Chronic stress seems to have taken the lead in our society as one of our number one emotions and has become one of the leading causes of disease. Change is the only inevitable thing in life so ask yourself what you are fighting against that is causing so much internal pressure and stress. Can you shift, go with the flow, and live in tune with what you really want? Anxiety is another sign that something is out of alignment and that your internal world does not match your external world. What can you change to bring them into alignment?

Release these emotions. You can do this in the presence of your horse and watch how he reacts to you becoming more aware and authentic. Can he help guide you? When your horse has a strong reaction to something consider that he may be reacting to your attitude. Step back and ask yourself what is happening internally for you. Be honest with yourself. With that state of mind, try again with your horse and see if you get a different response. We don't want to face our emotions because staying numb can be more comfortable. So instead we correct the horse and teach him to behave when we should possibly look within. Is the horse reacting to you in a way that others do in your life? Is this a pattern for you? Can the horse guide you to awaken something or become aware of an old story that no longer serves you?

We can start to work with the horse in a way that takes us on a journey to know ourselves and simultaneously train and empower the horse. When you have a strong reaction to something your horse does, good or bad, reflect on why you reacted in such a manner. Notice that it is a choice based on your perception. Is there another way to react? What is the underlying belief system at work here? How does this situation play out in the rest of your life? What is this a representation of?

Bring awareness to the situation. For example, if the horse "disobeying" makes you angry, ask yourself: Where else do you get angry when others disagree? How does that make them feel? If the horse walks away and it hurts your feelings, ask yourself: Who else walks away from you leaving you lonely? Could there be another explanation for their actions? If the horse does exactly what you want and you feel in control, ask yourself: Do you always need to be in control to feel safe? Who else are you controlling?

Utilize your time with the horse to uncover your underlying beliefs about life and training horses. For example, if your horse chooses to have a meltdown about something it gives you an opportunity to explore your inner landscape. Notice your reaction to the horse and work on those feelings to unlock a new way to relate to the horse and ultimately the world. You can ask yourself a series of questions:

- o What assumptions are you making based on your belief system?
- o Do those assumptions validate negative thoughts?
- o Do you feel the need to defend your position?
- o Are you blaming the horse?

- Are you criticizing yourself?
- Are you upset about your horse's behavior? Why or why not?
- What would happen if you just walked away from the activity that is causing the meltdown?
- If you walked away, would you feel defeated? Why or why not?
- Would walking away make you feel as though you weren't good enough or that the horse is bad?
- Why are you so attached to the outcome?
- What is the worst thing that could happen from doing something else?
- Would you feel like you lost control or respect?
- Could you change your perception to see that perhaps you gained control by choosing to walk away from a situation that was going to escalate and gained respect by giving respect rather than using force?

When you do not get the response you want from the horse it is easy to fall into negative thought. "I'm not good enough." "I'm a failure." "I can't do it." "This is stupid." "The horse is bad." "I give up." You need to recognize those thoughts, how they make you feel, and how the horse reacts. Try positive thinking and look for what is working and what is good. Don't blame or criticize the horse or yourself. Blaming the horse is not productive. If you have a plant that is struggling to grow, you change the way that you care for it and nourish it. Blaming the plant will not help it to stop wilting. Look inside yourself to find the key to change the horse's behavior. Look for the flaw in the method, the breakdown in communication, and the negative beliefs that are hindering you. Judge less and listen more.

We do not want our horses to resist or evade us, yet we often walk around in a cloud of negativity and all negativity is resistance.

When you look for how the horse is resisting or evading, you are in a pattern of thought that makes the horse your foe. The thing you are struggling with should not create conflict with the horse. Use it to illuminate the areas that you need to work on so that you can approach it from a different angle and strengthen your partnership. Even when you think you are clear it doesn't mean that it will be interpreted the way you intended. Remain flexible and creative to find new approaches to teaching the concept. Don't just wish that your horse would do something different because you will just attract more wishing. Expect him to succeed and see it in your mind.

Worrying creates a very detailed picture of what we don't want to have happen. Try using your time and imagination to create a detailed image of what you do want. Set yourself up for success rather than failure. When working with horses you have the added bonus that they think in pictures and can pick up on your energy. For example, if you worry about your horse spooking at the truck that is coming down the road your horse will likely deliver. Even if you think "don't spook" you are asking for it because there are no negatives in pictures – you are still creating an image of the spooking. Instead, try visualizing your horse standing with calm confidence as the truck passes and see what happens. With practice you will get better at controlling your thoughts when working with your horse.

You must have awareness of the internal and external so that you can see the cause and effect between them. Don't get absorbed or swept away by what the horse is doing or your emotions. They play on one another – your energy combines. Stay calm and centered and use your instinct to dance with the horse. Your perceptions, judgments, and opinions happen in the mind but the connection with the horse just is. To release the grip that your emotions or other's behaviors, including your horse's, have on you and no longer carry them around you have to really feel, process, and listen to them even if it's unpleasant. Don't just analyze them with your mind. The mind keeps you distant and labels your feelings, preventing you from embracing them and learning from them. It is the mind that interprets your emotions and the sensations in your body so if it is untrained and out of control, you are powerless to access your inner wisdom.

Following your intuition

Listen to your horse and work in collaboration with him. Let go of preconceived notions and plans set ahead of time. Be spontaneous, creative, and intuitive. Listen to your inner knowing. We all have wisdom and hold the answers within us but we must listen to be able to hear them. We all know how to work our way out. Ask the horse for support. The horse also holds wisdom but will, at times, need your support to work through the areas where he is stuck. Learn to be still and follow his lead so that you can guide one another to healing. Give your horse and yourself time to feel rather than just react. Build time and space into your training sessions to keep things from escalating. The horse will connect with you if you speak from your heart. To connect with him you must feel that you are worthy of, capable of, and deserving of that connection. If you fear love, partnership, or success you will always subconsciously sabotage the partnership.

When you are working with horses, rely on your personal insight and intuition. Intuition is about allowing yourself to follow some energetic cue that provides a knowing that you can feel, a gut instinct; not a knowing that you can intellectualize. It is a heart knowing rather than a mind knowing. Listening to intuition is trained out of us in favor of using reasoning skills and logic to make decisions and decide how to act. That inner knowing or instinct is feedback from the universe, or the horse, on an energetic level helping guide you to or away from things. It pays to listen. You may instinctually know how to "fix" an issue with the horse but if you get caught up in your head with what you've been taught and logical thinking, you may override your intuition.

Wisdom differs from knowledge. Wisdom cannot be taught; it is already within. Gather information and knowledge and never stop seeking to learn, but do so following your heart and not your intellect. Your heart holds many of the answers to working with horses and life in general. Trust your own truth. When you choose to deny your intuition is when you get led astray. Intuition is an internal, energetic knowledge. Horses, and most animals, rely on intuition as a primary source of information. Animals are often much more adept at reading energy and sensing information. Get out of your head and into your body so that you can feel it.

The horse can communicate with you on this level if you are open to it and practice this skill. The way to access it is through awareness and acceptance. Listen to the stirrings in your heart and awaken your soul. We are often closed off to the power of creativity and imagination. You have to trust the process and let the horse, who is already a master, share with you. As you learn to listen to your intuition, you may judge yourself or worry that others will judge you. It takes courage to choose to listen and trust to believe that what you hear is true. As you start to use intuition to receive information and intent to transmit it you may feel silly but the horse can give tangible proof of your power. As you believe in yourself more and practice this skill the horse will respond more readily to your feedback.

Staying present with patience

Life is about this moment. Is all of that chatter in your head really helping you connect with your horse? Is it helping you be a better person or live your life fully? Allow the horses to help you learn to live in the moment. Thoughts of the past are often connected to depression and thoughts of the future tend to be full of anxiety – happiness can only take place right now. When you become present you can connect to the horse and practice living in a state of awareness. As you get better at living your life, rather than stressing about things you have no control over, your life will become filled with joy, acceptance, and possibility. We need to change, become aware, and work on our inner landscape, which is then reflected in our outer world. Horses have the ability to engage fully with reality because they are not busy making up their own stories about it.

Interaction with the horse gives you a chance to work on this skill. In an ideal world you should end up in what is sometimes referred to as a "flow state" while working with your horse. You step into your bubble with him and leave all your worries and thoughts outside the gate. The world melts away and you are in a timeless state where nothing but you and the horse matters. Your energies combine and you work in harmony, blissfully unaware of anything else in the world or your life. It is just you and your horse. Both of you are in a heightened state of awareness with inner peace. You feel like you are able to conquer the world or accomplish anything in this moment. Just two creatures, fully empowered, collaborating, and dancing together with love and respect for your differences.

You must work in the moment without expectations of what is going to happen or demands of when you want it to happen. When you quiet the over-developed left side of your brain, you can awaken the receiving, intuitive right side to uncover new perceptions. When surrounded by silence and inner stillness you can listen to your heart and your horse. Join the horse where he lives – in the moment. Rather than dwelling on what just happened or the next thing you plan to do, just feel the moment. Be fully present. It is surprisingly hard to just experience the moment considering it is the only place we live. This moment is your life. Grasping for things to be different in the future won't save you, nor will worrying about the past. The past is gone and the future never arrives – they are both illusions of the mind.

This would be a good time to work on the art of doing nothing and processing how you feel. The barn can be your safe space to slow down and decompress. We are so rushed and hurried in our lives that we forget to slow down and enjoy what we're doing. If you go to the barn after work and are feeling rushed with a limited amount of time then it is hard to fully tune in to the horse. Set a fifteen minute warning alarm so that you can just let things unfold without worrying about how much you can get done before you need to leave. When the alarm goes off you know it is time to wrap up what you are doing and put your horse away. Enjoy the time you have with your horse and stay fully present. See how fortunate you are to be having this experience without the stress of time. If you don't have a lot of time, don't sacrifice the quality of time you do have by feeling rushed. When you are rushed it makes the horse nervous.

Simplify. Learn to relax and take it easy with your horse. We live in a fast paced culture where time is money. We often feel that we have to be doing something and aren't comfortable just being. It does not make you a bad person if you do "nothing" on occasion. We are often too hurried in our tasks with horses. Slow down, breathe, and act as though you have all the time in the world to accomplish a task. The horse has no agenda. The horse is simply a horse and a present reflection of his surroundings. Horses are happy to just stand under a shade tree and enjoy life. It is the human that feels as though she has to be doing something, accomplishing something. Horses understand the ancient art of doing nothing and it's alright to try doing nothing with them.

The art of doing nothing does not mean that you sit like a lump and let your mind wander in endless loops. It is the practice of being present, aware, and living in the moment. How can you expect to truly know and understand your horse, and him you, if the only time you spend with him is barking orders or imposing your ideas on him. Just be present and observe his tendencies. Quality friendships are built on being there for one another, listening, and spending time together. Herds of horses are with each other 24/7 and rely on that close knit bond for support. If you only spend an hour a week with your horse you can't build depth into your partnership. You must be there reliably. Don't just plan time to ride; also plan for time to hang out with him and his herd.

If the only time you spend with your horse is to benefit yourself then you can never have a partnership. If you only ever approach your horse with the expectation of doing something to him or having him work for you he will grow to resent it rather than look forward to seeing you. So spend time with your horse in a genuine way. If you only spend time with him for selfish reasons then it is futile.

When you do bring him in you don't always have to do something. You can bring him in for a carrot and then turn him back out. Not everything has to revolve around work. Take the stress out of it, make it enjoyable for both of you, and keep your horse guessing. Spend time doing some massage on your horse, take him for a walk to graze, turn him lose in the arena, teach him a trick, dance and play with him, sit in the field and hang out with him, scratch his itches, or go splash in a creek. Enjoy your horse.

One of my favorite things to do ever since I was a child is to go out into the pasture at night and climb up onto my horse's back and just hang out with him as he grazes. Or, if your horse isn't that calm, just sit with the herd under the stars. The barn is a different place at night. It feels magical and is my favorite time to go and hang out with the horses. Maybe because I can't see as well the smells are stronger, the air is crisper, and the sound of the horses breathing, chewing, and walking around is more beautiful. At night your awareness is greater, you're on alert, and you can better sense your surroundings. Remember horses see in the dark much better than we do so they won't be spooked by you moving through the darkness. Though they can see you, they may be confused that you are encroaching on a human-free hour of the day.

You can use grooming as a tool for awareness and bonding. It is a beneficial healing exercise for both of you. Don't let grooming be something that you have to get through in order to ride. You can use it as a somatic awareness activity that helps you connect with the horse and build relationship. Use the flow and rhythm of grooming, particularly brushing, to calm your mind and center you. Take the time that you are grooming to carve out a space inside you that can be a well of patience, understanding, and empathy to use in the arena. Long, firm, calming strokes in combination with deep breathing can really help the horse relax and settle. The use of bodywork and touch helps the horse feel good, centered, and aware of his body which is exactly the state you want when you climb onto his back.

Also, don't have other people groom your horse for you prior to riding. Grooming is an essential part of the process to build your partnership and prepare for, or recover from, work. Just as all people have different moods every day, the horse that you rode yesterday may not be the horse you are about to get on. When you groom him you have a chance to see if he is sensitive today or if he feels sore or grouchy or frisky. If you groom your horse every day it gives you a chance to pick up on subtle changes. Spend time with him before you start asking for work. Jumping straight into training, or a ride, is rude. You can also use grooming as an exercise in trust and communication by not restricting or tying him for the grooming and tacking session.

Taking your time also benefits your training. The best way for your horse to work and learn is in a relaxed state. As soon as the horse starts to get tense, nervous, or worried his head goes up and his body stiffens. In this state he is prepared to flee and looking for an escape route rather than listening to you and assimilating training. Back off and release the pressure. Walk away if you have to and let the horse settle. Only resume work if he can remain in a calm and relaxed state. Horses are not good at pushing through but do understand an approach and retreat method.

Focus on breath work, moving slowly, and staying present. This is a good break from our lives and allows the horse to relax. You may accomplish less but what you do accomplish will be positive and retained and integrated better. Breathing, in particular, is an excellent tool that is always available to us. Many spiritual practices teach the importance of the breath as a way to quiet the mind and find the moment. Inspiration is all about breathing and working with spirit in the moment. Each breath is an opportunity to find your center. When you are inspired you are full of breath, full of spirit, and full of creativity. Your horse will also pick up on the rhythm of your breathing. If you are nervous then you will take quick, shallow breaths and the horse will do the same. However, if you take deep breaths and relax your body the horse will mirror you and relax.

It is perfectly acceptable to take a break in a training session. If you are facing fear issues or stress you can call a time out for yourself to literally take a breather. Do breathing exercises, meditate, or take a walk. The horse won't mind. If you are stressed, tense, or cautious you will just feed that energy to your horse. Ground yourself, find your center, and find a way to return to the work in a way that allows you both to feel successful. What is good for the horse is good for you. Don't let your fear or frustration get the best of you. I think one of the primary reasons riders lash out at their horses is that they start to feel unsafe and the predator "I'm going to get you" switch gets flipped. Diffuse the situation, break down the issue into bite-sized pieces, and try again with good communication and a clear head. This is a great skill to carry into life.

Training involves infinite patience and tiny steps. It is about the journey and experiencing the moment. You can't push either of you faster than what you can do together as a team. There will be peaks and valleys in training, days when you make a lot of progress, and times you feel stuck. Take time to work through the sticky parts because you will find a key or important piece that will help you in the future. If you're only focused on the outcome then you will miss the chance to celebrate the thousands of successes you had along the way. Life is about the journey, not the destination. Once you reach the destination you are still you and the horse is still the horse. Would you rather arrive competition-ready with a true partnership or a defeated horse that follows commands?

It is time to quiet the mind and become physically and emotionally aware of yourself and the horse. You still don't need an agenda or a plan for training. Look at the horse as a mirror of your heart and soul and connect on a deeper level. You started to build compassion, confidence, trust, forgiveness, and playfulness. Allow that to soak in without expectations. It is time to make a heart connection which means that you have to quiet the ego to hear your emotions and follow your intuition. This is a chance to listen to yourself, the horse, and the vibrations of the universe to begin unlocking your inner wisdom and beauty.

You need to look deep within yourself to see what old thoughts, patterns, and behaviors are holding you back. At times it can seem as though they are the absolute truth because they are so ingrained but it is possible to change over time. Your feelings arise based on the way that you view things. Mindfulness is the key to see the beliefs you hold about yourself, your relationships, your culture, and the world. You must be willing to change your addictive thought patterns and inaccurate perceptions. If you don't like them then believe something else and change your life. For example, it is the belief that you are not worthy or good enough that gives you the "go ahead" when you decide to reach for another drink, piece of cake, or cigarette. If you become aware of these moments and decide that isn't working for you then you can connect with spirit instead of acting in a way that your soul knows is bad for your body. This is a form of incongruence. You are not powerless.

Life is a journey through the unknown and requires a certain amount of faith and vulnerability. You only have control over yourself – your thoughts, perception, and actions. You can only make choices in the moment. If you have not learned to harness the power of your mind, which in turn determines your actions, reactions, and ultimately your destiny then you have no control over anything. This leaves you without power or purpose where you are swept away by ego rather than living centered in your greatness. If you have no control then life becomes a terrifying thing that happens to you. If you find inner stillness, life becomes a beautiful experience that you help to co-create and facilitate. With awareness you can begin living, creating, and feeling positive about your life. Endless possibilities and opportunities become available and you no longer need to struggle to shape the external circumstances of your life. You can surrender to the unknown because you know and trust yourself.

CHAPTER FIVE:
INTENTIONAL COMMUNICATION

Intent: *directed with keen attention; having the mind or will concentrated on some end purpose*
Communication*: an act of transmitting; an exchange of information or opinions*

All solid relationships hinge on good communication. Once you have taken the time to build confidence and awareness you are ready to start building your communication skills with the horse. You cannot have a positive impact on the horse's movement until you have built an understandable language between horse and human. Clear communication is the key to begin moving the horse's feet and building the skills required for your specific discipline. The time spent unraveling past experiences, observing and playing with the horse, and developing emotional awareness is critical to approaching communication with a new perspective. Learning to communicate through intuition and intention is the next step to building an empowered partnership.

The need for a common language

Horsemanship is a bit like creating two whole new languages that are based on neither the human's nor the horse's native tongue: the language you use on the ground and the language you use on his back. With energy and intent you can create overlap between the two, but there still has to be some level of translation when you move from the ground to his back. When it comes to riding, the only natural instinct for the horse is to buck off the predator. Aids and tools, natural or not, have no innate meaning – just as letters on a page have no meaning if you don't speak the language. You must teach the horse what the aids mean.

Humans are very verbal creatures. We rarely have silence in our lives and are inundated with an internal dialogue, language, and spoken communication from television, telephones, text messaging, social networking, reading, writing, talking, and the constant dialogue in our minds. We are vocal, thinking beings. The horse does not have spoken language or words. He is a feeling, sensing, moving being who dwells in silence. The horse is unable to understand our complex reasoning or communicate with us in a way we are most comfortable. He is not adept at understanding and distinguishing sounds.

The vocal nature of humans and the silent nature of horses can be a big hurdle to overcome. We have to learn to relate in a new manner or we will miss out on the feedback from our horses. For example, horses are silent even when in pain. If your horse were to yelp like a dog when you dug your spurs in, would you react differently? I know when I accidentally step on a dog paw, eliciting a sharp yelp, I jump a mile and then apologize profusely. You know the scream of the unhappy, restrained cat? What if your horse did that when you pulled really hard on the bit? What if your horse whimpered with nerves when you placed your ill-fitting saddle on his back? Would you then know that you were causing pain and change your behavior? We have to learn to feel empathy based on non-vocal feedback from the horse by staying in touch with our bodies.

Becoming aware of your body language and waves of emotion will help you in all your relationships. Even though we are often unaware of it due to our obsession with spoken language, we communicate primarily through body language and we are constantly reading others' energy at a subconscious level. As you learn to communicate more deliberately through body language you have the opportunity to take the mind, and therefore the ego, out of the equation. Quiet the mind and communicate with the horse through the body as directed by the soul. This is a new way of communicating for many people and is not focused on what you know or think. Words are powerful but actions speak louder than words. Your actions show who you really are and that is what the horse reads.

The horse has a larger and stronger energy field around him than we do, through which he relates to the world. The horse is very good at transmitting energy as a way of communicating. Though the horse tends to be silent, he actually has a fairly complex and intricate form of body language. His lips, nostrils, eyes, ears, head carriage, posture, and tail are always speaking to you and can be very dynamic and easy to read. We all know that pinned ears and bared teeth mean "back off". His body sends us signals about his inner state and emotions. As you become more astute you will look at the whole body for subtle tension, weight shifts, and the way he holds his ribs as signals.

While we can train ourselves to better read the horse, we will never be perfect at understanding, or even seeing, each little movement that holds meaning. Horses have the ability to make such tiny shifts that it is almost unperceivable to the human. For example, the horse has a muscle under the skin that allows him to quiver his skin in the precise spot that a fly landed. He can actually hold tension in his skin which is not something that humans cannot do. We will never be able to speak horse or actually become the "lead mare" because, just as our spoken language is too complex for them to understand, their body language is too complex for us. We cannot swivel our ears or swish our tail – we don't even have a tail.

Working with the horse on the ground is all about body language and visual cues. When you move into the saddle, communication changes to one of feel and touch – a foreign concept for both horse and human. Neither of you actually knows how to converse based on touch being applied to different areas of the body. We use touch to express love and warmth, not to hold conversation and communicate requests.

Physical cues are a very one-sided form of communication because it involves the rider applying pressure to an area of the horse's body and expecting a response. The horse is not expected to respond by touching the human. They are left to simply react. We then judge that reaction as right or wrong and punish or reward the horse accordingly. Our only form of listening on the horse is to feel what they are doing and to determine whether it is an adequate response to our request. This is not reciprocal, collaborative communication.

The most successful horsemen have put in the time to learn about the horse from the horse. You must be willing to put in the time and effort to learn communication skills from the horse. It takes time in the barn and in the saddle. Of course input from others can help shorten the learning curve, but don't rely solely on that. You can't learn feel, timing, kindness, trust, or respect from a book, video, or instructor. You discover those things within you through guidance from the horse.

Humans find it harder than horses to learn to communicate through intuition, intent, concentration, visualization, and energy. Be gentle with yourself but persevere. You must catch the negative thoughts and limiting beliefs that are swirling around in your head and trust the process. It is one of the greatest feelings when you start to grasp this concept and begin acting as one with the horse. By using your intent and feeling to communicate, your body naturally responds in subtle ways. Your thoughts and emotions show up in your body and the horse can pick up on that and respond. You can even use it for more advanced things like visualizing more flexion in the hind limbs while riding a collected trot. It's that simple and magical but it is so hard for humans because we are caught up in the drama in our heads.

The horse, in part, mirrors your emotions because he can sense and feel them himself. Most riders come to understand that if they are nervous it will cause the horse to be nervous, but it also works with feeling confident. If we know a horse will spook at something with such certainty that we feel it to our core, the horse is bound to spook. However, if we want the horse to halt square on X and doubt it will happen it won't happen. Riding and communication would happen effortlessly if we could learn to muster certainty, with the emotion to back it up, that the horse will do what we are asking.

If your mind and your body are busy then you are just communicating loud noise to your horse and he will learn to tune you out. The horse is not able to pick out one thought from a constant stream of thoughts or one shift in weight from a body that is never still. Silence gives rise to intent through which you can access the power of pure potential. Intention has energy, power, and emotion behind it. The clarity of your intention equates to the quality of movement that you will receive from the horse.

Don't be afraid to try new approaches. The horse will respond positively when you start to get it right. You need to develop patience for yourself and the horse because you both have a learning curve. It is up to you to figure out how to make the necessary changes in yourself to have the horse work with you willingly. Be impeccable with your words and your actions.

To do that you need to silence your mind and be in touch with your body and your emotions. Allow your feelings to flow through you and see if they generate a response in the horse. When you allow things to just unfold without attachment or resistance to the outcome, you can observe the ways in which your inner world shapes your outer world. Awareness is the brush that paints our desires on the canvas of our life and there are infinite possibilities of creation.

Exploration of communication on the ground

You have to believe in yourself and develop the confidence in your ability to communicate effectively though your intentions. You will make mistakes initially so don't be afraid to laugh at yourself and learn from them. Safety must come first but don't take your riding too seriously. Remember to keep playing with the horse and relying on his feedback. Communication goes both ways so you are sharing the ideas, knowledge, and opinions of both horse and human. Both partners must be heard and respected. You must be willing to listen and be attuned to the energy and messages that your horse gives you.

Do not use your intention to control the horse and get what you want. It is a communicated request that enables you to guide the horse to inspiration and empowerment. Intent should be communicated with grace and ease. You must take responsibility for what and how you are communicating. You should never use your innate power and wisdom to work against your horse. Work with him in harmony.

Prior to training a new skill ask yourself if you and the horse are physically ready as well as mentally and emotionally prepared. The horse cannot be successful if he is not prepared on all levels to be able and willing to choose to respond to your input easily and happily. Sometimes your horse's actions will be less skillful. Just acknowledge it and keep working to move forward without beating yourself up. New exercises will be a little rocky and uncoordinated at first. That's okay too. Refinement comes later after both of you have learned the move and the communication that goes along with it. At first it is not about perfection; it's about effort. If you want the horse to move forward, feel successful when he moves forward and worry about the speed, direction, gait, cadence, and straightness later. Teach one thing at a time.

The premise of most horse training is to have the horse yield to pressure but horses don't necessarily yield to pressure naturally. They may actually move into it if they feel threatened or as though they cannot escape. So we must teach them to yield by applying pressure and immediately releasing it and rewarding the horse for the correct response. Be sure the request is fair and clear and don't fight the horse. Only reward the desired response or you will train the wrong outcome.

Horses learn by trial and error and they don't always know what we want. When you give a horse a cue to do something for the first time it is a bit like throwing out a word in German with no context or dictionary. "Danke". The horse has no way to translate what that means. Therefore it is important to be as clear as possible with your intention and reward the effort even if it is not the right response at first. The horse tries something in response to your request which is a bit like guessing what the definition of the word is based on an infinite number of possibilities. If he guesses the wrong definition it does not help to say "NO! DANKE!". That doesn't clarify what the word means and will discourage him from wanting to figure it out.

You must stay clear and not punish the horse as he works out the answer. You have to help the horse navigate that and encourage closer and closer approximations to the answer until he finally gets it. Be sure to reward him very clearly when you get the response that you want. Getting it once doesn't mean the horse knows it but he will get to the answer faster next time. Once he understands a concept he will want to play with it. If it feels good, he will want to explore the dynamics of it. Give him space to do this. He is not being disobedient - he is finding his own self-awareness and exploring the new activity.

Horses learn quickly, without repetition, and have amazing memories. Don't drill them endlessly and be careful not to teach the wrong response. It will take longer to undo bad training than to progress slowly with good training. The response doesn't have to be perfect. You are just looking for effort in the right direction, even if that means a shift of weight. That is progress. Give the horse plenty of time to contemplate between requests. Soak time is more important than the number of times you ask for him to yield.

When first teaching a response to a cue it is all about patience. You don't need to escalate the amount of pressure you use rapidly. Ask and give the horse time to process. If you don't get a response, ask with more clarity. If your horse reacts in the wrong way, continue with that amount of pressure and help the horse figure out what you want. Don't just start applying more and more pressure to demand a response if the horse doesn't understand what you are asking.

Use the lightest amount of pressure that you can muster – just a flicker of energy and then breathe. Give the horse a chance to respond or offer a behavior and then ask again and breathe. Focus on the space between the requests. In an ideal world, you should think "walk", the horse walks and that's the end of it without any need to continue asking for walk. If you feel as though he is going to stop you simply think "walk" again to confirm that you are still walking. Music would just be noise if it weren't for the space between the notes. Give the horse space to make music not noise.

Release the tension when you get the slightest indication the horse is beginning to respond in the way you want. Working with horses is not about immediate results. He must get to the point that he understands what you are asking, without getting worked up in the process, and then you can work on faster responses. How quickly the horse responds to a cue has more to do with the rider's timing than the horse's timing. How soft can you ask and how quick can you release? Be understanding and understandable.

If you use equipment, gadgets, or quick fix methods to gain a certain look or achieve the outcome faster, you are not giving the horse the freedom to discover self-carriage and empowerment. Instead of forcing an outcome, channel the energy of your horse and direct that energy slowly where you want it to go. You can think of training a horse as being similar to spinning a pot of clay. You start with a vision of what you would like the lump of clay to become and with a little pressure here and a light touch there you can mold it into a beautiful masterpiece. Training should not be based on making the wrong thing uncomfortable and the right thing comfortable. It is about blocking the energy you don't want and allowing the energy you do want, a process that requires timing, feel, and awareness. Encouraging the horse to develop is a softer approach that allows choice.

Everything that you do on the horse's back you should first do on the ground where you can be much clearer about your signals, you can see one another, and you are in a less vulnerable position. As you play with your horse he will start focusing on you and seeking communication with you. This is your opening to begin making suggestions about what to do next and start influencing his movement. Out of the awareness that you built you can start by emanating the feeling of what you would like the horse to do. Your intention and feelings mold your body language so, if those are clear, your body will naturally move and the horse will understand.

You can learn to utilize body language while working with horses on the ground and they can learn to understand what you want. Remember that initially flapping your arms, pointing your fingers, or bending at the waist doesn't have any meaning to them. We have a completely different body structure and movement. What they really read are the things they understand, such as your eyes, your breathing patterns, the tension in your body, and your energy. That is what we should learn to communicate through by using our intuition to read those things in the horse and intention to communicate them to the horse.

Start out with simple exercises like learning to push the horse away or draw him in with your energy field. Don't use physical contact or equipment to help you. See the difference between using hard, concentrated vision versus soft, unfocused vision. Staring at the horse will often drive him away. Try tightening your core to send him away and softening it to bring him closer. Dance with the horse. Learn to interact through pressure and release to lead and be led through energy. When both of you choose to interact in this way you begin developing communication that is polite, respectful, gentle, and subtle. You start to communicate in a way the horse understands and you transcend the need to bark orders because you are being heard and, in return, you are listening. A conversation develops from the heart. You are not just communicating requests; rather, you are sharing your energy, your pleasure, and your desires.

When you give your horse a cue, wait and see how he reacts. Stay in touch with your inner self. How are you reacting to the way he is reacting? In turn, how does that make him react? A conversation can only happen in the moment, like everything else. Stay aware. How often do you repeat past conversations in your head or practice a conversation you are anticipating? Horses can help you learn to converse in the present moment so that you can respond authentically and say what you mean, think, and feel without making a quip that you regret. They can teach you to build space into the conversation so that you aren't left thinking "I wish I had said X" or "I wish I hadn't said X".

This method of communication also means that you don't have to think about every way a conversation could go in the future. You can't predict what another person will say, or what the horse will do, but if you trust yourself and your communication skills, you will have the confidence to know that you will say the right thing in the moment when the moment comes. You must stay detached from the outcome because you can't control how another will respond. As long as you stay calm, clear, and true to yourself, their reaction will be their responsibility and not a reflection of you. The horse can help teach you when someone else's reactions are a reflection of you and when they are a reflection of that person's perspective. Stop and listen, don't anticipate the next step in the conversation, allow it to flow, and don't be afraid of silence.

Bring mindfulness into all of your activities with the horse so that you can learn to communicate and listen. For example, lunge work should never be a mindless activity that entails driving the horse in circles around you. It is a chance to connect and reflect so that you can practice communication to begin teaching the horse the skill of self-carriage. Be sure to always give plenty of breaks, changes of direction, and encouragement. Ultimately you want to build up to free lunging the horse in a circle around you. This is not about moving his feet to prove that you can dominate him. When free lunging, the horse is literally free to leave, meaning he is making a choice to work with you because it is of benefit to him. You are there to help him learn to become physically and emotionally balanced. It is also a great way for you to learn about yourself. Work together and teach each other.

You can also utilize mirroring if you get stuck on something by modeling it in your body. For example, if you are teaching side pass and your horse is shuffling sideways rather than crossing his legs over, you can exaggeratedly cross your legs and show the horse what you are looking for. In this way you can model behavior and emotional states to help your horse figure out what is expected of him.

Translating groundwork to the ridden aids

As we move from the ground to their back, we can take the work that we have done building communication through intent, intuition, and an exchange of energy and use it to translate yet another set of communication skills. The goal is to create less demanding physical pressure and more intent-based suggestions. Instead of spurs use concentrated sight. You want to be able to "whisper" a clear, concise message and then release pressure as the reward to celebrate both of your successes. You want to get to the point that a shift of your weight on or off the horse, clear intent, vision, and light touch are all that is needed to communicate your desires. Physical cues are used for back-up to internal cues, and your tools should be used merely as an extension of your body to help clarify your requests.

It is impossible to learn good timing and feel if you are unbalanced in the saddle. Work on timing and feel on the ground and, if needed, work with a solid horse separately to learn balance and confidence in the tack. You must learn to do nothing before learning to do something. The rider needs to know how to sit in the saddle without having an effect on the horse. Until you learn to not interfere with the horse you cannot be effective at communicating with the horse. Start with the most basic things and build up to learn to control your body and let it go with the movement of the horse. Each body part needs to move separately to develop an independent seat.

The goal should be relaxation for the horse and rider. You want soft, fluid, supple muscles and a calm attitude. All of the "bad" things a horse does, whether it's running through the reins, being slow off your leg, spooking, or bucking, come from tension. That tension could be physical, mental, or emotional. If you want the horse to stay soft, supple, calm, and relaxed then you must do the same. You cannot become rigid or tense and expect your horse to work in a state of relaxation. It also means that your equipment, such as the saddle, cannot cause pain or restrict movement, nor can you work your horse to a state of exhaustion. He must stay in a state of comfort. Work done with tension is not valuable so you are better off not breaking his trust and teaching him to be defensive. When tension arises, slow down, go back to basics, take a break, or solve the problem.

If you want your horse to be supple and giving you cannot snatch the reins or hit him in the mouth accidentally. This is confusing for the horse and will cause him to brace in response to, and eventually in anticipation of, discomfort. You should always maintain a soft and elastic feel. Contact is all about feeling what the horse is doing so that you can communicate effectively. You cannot feel anything if you are tense. Your hands should always be light, giving, and sensing rather than tense, restrictive, and telling. Sloppy, lazy hands that are too loose can also become harsh and they do not give you the ability to feel. You also feel through your seat and legs. Your legs should just rest on the horse's side and not grip for dear life. Do not try to hold your position. Relax into your body, arms, and legs and surrender to the movement with balance. Your body should be like a rubber band absorbing energy and not a ping pong ball bouncing around on top of the horse.

One way to flawlessly communicate when riding is to work with the natural rhythm of the horse and your body. You have to allow the motion of your horse's back. When we become nervous or unbalanced we block the natural movement of the horse. Allow the horse to move you as he moves. Stay fluid and balanced to feel the timing of when to encourage the horse. Get in touch with the horse and follow your intuition. You will get moments of connection and harmony and you must celebrate these. If you focus on retaining these moments, you are all but guaranteed not to achieve them. With practice you will be able to sustain that blissful feeling longer.

You can also use the power of positive thinking and visualization to help you communicate with the horse. Look where you want to go, both literally and figuratively. But, in the same way you can't prove a negative, you can't think about what you *don't* want to have happen. For example, let's say you are working a horse in the half of the arena away from the gate and every time you cross the center of the arena, he throws his shoulder and tries to make a beeline for the gate. If you ride toward the point at which you are going to cross the arena thinking about how he does this, what it feels like, wondering if he will actually succeed this time, and anticipating that he is going to do it again then you are actually sending the signal "throw your shoulder and run like hell when we get to X".

That is not what you want but by focusing on it and visualizing it you are sending your horse the picture of the behavior that you would really rather avoid. This is where staying in the moment, mindfulness, awareness, and clear intention becomes important. The last loop around the arena is already past and you corrected or blocked the behavior as it happened so let that go. Ride the current stride and bring your attention to what you are doing right now. So as you ride across the center of the arena, focus on a nice bend and where you will meet the rail again. Your eyes and *intention* are on successfully executing the turn while your awareness and *attention* are on the current stride and what your horse is doing in the moment.

Leave the past in the past and don't anticipate what may happen in the future. Feel what is happening in your horse right now, which will allow you to make a timely and accurate adjustment if he starts to throw a shoulder without the need to plan for "what if he throws his shoulder?" Simply feel what is here and now in the moment with your desire and intention a few strides out completing the task successfully. Of course, when he is successful he needs to be immediately rewarded. Perhaps a scratch on the withers as you fall nicely in line with the rail as an acknowledgement for the effort that was made. Or maybe a downward transition to walk and letting him have a loose rein. The loose rein will allow him to relax and show that you trust that he isn't going to "take advantage" and try to head for the gate. If your horse is consistently trying to run for home then it means that he is not enjoying or engaged in his work and an effort should be made to change the situation, not just manage the behavior, so that you once again have a willing partner.

Physical cues are used for clarification and to encourage the horse to act on your intent. In the same way that you use your energy to move the horse on the ground, you can use it in the saddle. Try using your legs and seat through energy rather than muscles. The body blocks and allows energy to channel the horse's movement in the desired direction. Physical aids are not demands or punishments but a way to actually aid the horse. They should be a suggestion that encourages the horse to try and then they must allow the horse to act.

It is important to teach the horse that physical touches in different places have different meanings. Start out with more exaggerated aids that are spread out to make it clear the difference between bend, move over, move forward, lift, shoulder over, and hip over.

If you only use your leg in the same spot the horse will become confused and not know how to respond. With green horses these movements are more drastic which means making a bigger movement, not applying more pressure. As the horse learns the meaning of your requests, you can refine the aids to become more subtle. The green horse needs more guidance and support the way a first grader needs more help to sound out words than a sixth grader. However, the sixth grader may still need that extra support when learning a new or complicated task.

Think about your aids as releasing pressure rather than adding it. Don't put on a stronger leg. Take your leg off and then let it sit back on the horse's side. In this way you make a suggestion rather than a command. It will also prevent him from bracing his muscles against the tension that you are generating. If you first ask by releasing pressure then you can apply light pressure for clarification or as a correction.

Aids should be applied and released within the same stride to help the horse. Use the rhythm of the stride to be effective and ensure that there is space between requests. If you never release the aid then you are essentially nagging the horse and he will become dull to your requests. The horse also can't respond to multiple requests at once, but he can respond to requests made in quick succession. To do that you must be clear and learn coordination, which takes time and practice.

Riding is not about pushing the horse off the aids. For example, if you want a leg yield then the slight, gentle physical cues will happen naturally if you focus your energy correctly. Ride from your center and your legs and hands will follow. Imagine that you have a light shooting out of your belly button, from your center, like a flashlight. Shine the light where you want to go and your body naturally will apply the correct aids. For example, to turn right you would engage your core to shine your light to the right.

This naturally opens your right hand and leg, closes your left hand and leg, and engages your seat aids. This method will keep you from applying harsh, stiff, or mechanical aids. Use your balance and weight to help the horse move by opening and closing space to guide him. Also use your eyes and your vision. You will end up where you're looking.

In addition, for the horse to yield one way the other side has to create room for him to move into. Open a space with the opposite leg to allow movement or the horse will meet resistance and become confused and frustrated. This results in the horse hollowing out, scooting forward, or resisting. You haven't given him the space to yield into so he tries to move away in a different direction. This isn't the horse disobeying – it is the rider being ineffective. You are the one who needs to change, allow, and become fluid.

Learn to ride off your body rather than off your hands. A turn doesn't require pulling the horse around with your inside hand. Rather, your inside leg creates bend and your outside rein helps support the horse and blocks him from drifting out. You don't need to pull or push the horse anywhere with your aids – you guide and support him.

Don't give your horse something to lean against. Teach him to carry and balance himself. Resistance creates more resistance and the horse will always win a pulling or pushing match. When your horse pulls you can push and turn his energy into your idea rather than fighting against him. When he pushes, pull. If the horse throws his hind quarters to the inside he is pushing against you. Rather than pushing him back into straightness use that energy and pull the hind quarters over further to do a few steps of haunches in. If the horse pulls away from you on the ground, don't pull him back toward you. Push him with your energy and do some side pass. Don't fight the horse. Initially go with him and later you can begin to correct things.

When you apply pressure, whether though a leg aid, your hand, or your energy, it should pulse or vibrate. You can use less force if pressure is intermittent. It is easy to ignore a finger placed on your shoulder. It is harder to ignore tapping on your shoulder – generated by removing and applying touch – or nudging – where the contact remains but intermittent pressure is applied. It is possible to adjust to accepting much more significant force if it is steady and not pulsating. This does not mean that you kick the horse rather than squeeze. The goal is to be as gentle as possible.

The stronger your aids are, the more rigid the horse will be. Let's say you want the horse to yield his ribs as you would in a bend or a lateral movement. A kick or spur to the side is going to be counterproductive. You need him to stay soft and fluid to complete the task. Think about your reaction if someone punches you in the stomach. You not only strongly contract your stomach muscles but also tense the rest of your body. A kick will cause the horse to brace against you to protect himself rather than remaining soft and fluid enough to effectively yield his ribs. Discomfort will cause resistance.

If you are struggling, find ways on his back to translate what you are asking. If you want the horse to canter you could ride around the ring smacking or spurring or clucking. If you want to do away with that type of training, use something the horse understands while applying light, clear, gentle canter aids. Have someone cue the horse from the ground or ride with someone and allow your horse to follow the other horse into canter. You don't want these things to become a crutch but, because the horse understands those things, you can pair them with the new, strange leg and seat aids to obtain the desired result in a nonthreatening way. Another great method is through play or a game where the canter will happen naturally out of your enthusiasm to go faster. Or go out for a trail ride where you have lots of open space and it is easier for the horse. Some people might not feel comfortable with that but, by the time you are teaching canter, you should have a reliable halt.

Traditionally it is believed that the horse should continue at the speed and direction that the rider determined without fail until he is told otherwise. However, if you are encouraging the horse to really listen to what you want and you start anticipating the next move, are off balance, or start thinking about what you don't want then you are sending him mixed signals. Then you have to ask yourself if his change of direction or speed was due to something you did. He does not deserve to be corrected if he is reading you – precisely what you have been encouraging him to do!

As you find balance, you can start using more intent-based cues and fewer physical cues, but your horse will stop offering to listen if you continue to "yell" at him by mistake. How discouraging is it when you sit down to do something at work and someone immediately comes in to nag you about getting that task done. It would be better if they saw that you were preparing to work on it and gave you a "thank you" instead of harping on it. Recognizing the effort with good timing is critical and creates a soft, responsive horse with slight aids. If you are in tune with the energy and vibration of your horse it will also serve to help you predict a spook or a shoulder falling in. The same way that the horse can feel your intent, you can learn to feel his.

Communicating rewards and corrections

You aren't just communicating commands but also rewards, corrections, pleasure, and displeasure. There will be times when you need to correct the horse's behavior. A correction says "Good effort but maybe try it this way, good boy" whereas a punishment says "Wrong, bad horse. You stupid idiot – get it right, damn it!" State a correction in a positive way that builds partnership instead of a punitive way that destroys partnership. A leader corrects and guides the horse to success. When you grow frustrated it is a sign that you are no longer communicating effectively, not that the horse is doing anything wrong, so don't punish him out of your frustration. When a correction is made it should not go on endlessly. You must react in a timely manner to the transgression, make it clear that behavior is not okay, and then forget it and move on. Control your anger and don't hound the horse.

If a correction is not clear, it can lead to confusion, resentment, and fear. The correction has no meaning if you are just manhandling the horse. When making a correction use speed and agility to gain respect instead of force. If you are typically quiet when working with the horse then a sharp vocal noise is a strong correction without having to get physical. Timing is everything so you must be aware and sure of yourself to act in a swift, fair manner at the right moment to indicate your displeasure. Do not hesitate. Trust yourself and act with authority. Mistakes may happen but as long as you are kind and well-intentioned the horse has an endless supply of forgiveness and try.

Look for ways to reward the horse, rather than punish. You want to try to increase success and find things to celebrate instead of managing failures. Instead of asking what's wrong, ask what's right and be sure to reward the effort and not the outcome. Help the horse to be successful and remember that his version of success may not always be your definition of success. You should always remain positive if the horse is trying. You don't want to shut down his learning process, creativity, trust, and will. Initially, rewards must be timed impeccably to make clear the response that you want. Over time you can begin to reward intermittently to reinforce the behavior and strengthen the response.

We tend to use negative reinforcement, where we remove something unpleasant as a reward, as the primary reward system when training horses. We apply pressure to ask for a cue and the reward for trying is to release the pressure. This means that you can't continually apply pressure, whether it is your seat, leg, hand, intention, or energy, or the horse will end up in a shutdown state because he can't ever get away from the pressure. Positive reinforcement training, where the horse receives something desirable as a reward, needs to be used more in horse training.

Positive reinforcement is harder to use because the horse naturally has what he needs. As predators we must create a plan and go on a hunt to receive the reward of food but horses just have to put their heads down to graze. Whether using positive or negative reinforcement, the work itself and the horse's connection with the rider should ultimately become rewarding in and of itself. Discovering a new way to move, unlocking his power, and finding new ways to connect and communicate are important to the horse and can become incentives.

Some people are working with clicker training but that isn't always practical as it requires a strong, motivating reward. In general, a well-timed rub, release of pressure, or a lump of sugar will suffice. It is important to know your horse and what he finds rewarding. Most horses don't enjoy being patted and some are uncomfortable being touched or scratched on certain areas of their body. For example, if you were to rub a head shy horse's face as a reward he may read it as punitive while others love to have their face rubbed. Sometimes I use really drastic rewards like hopping off for the day when my horse has a major breakthrough, rather than continuing to try for perfection. It's okay to sometimes spontaneously end a session much sooner than usual but you can't use it all the time. It's a bit like getting to go home from work early on a Friday in recognition of finishing a big project.

You can actually reward your horse by feeling positive and joyful. Send him positive emotions when he tries hard and he too will feel good about the work you are doing. The horse will work with you and do things he wouldn't do on his own if it makes him feel good. Part of that comes from you feeling good and really enjoying the work. As you feel more empowered riding him, he will feel more empowered. That means that you must remember why you love riding and why you love your horse. Be grateful for the opportunity and celebrate the successes rather than looking for and trying to correct the faults.

Balancing the amount you ask for, the type of reward, and how much effort will earn the reward can be hard to do. Don't ask for big leaps in concepts. If you want the horse to be successful you must take baby steps. Not all horses are equally motivated by the same rewards or interested in work, so use a variety of approaches to learn what your horse likes best. Reserve his favorite reward for big tries and breakthroughs in training. Ask for progressively more. At first a shift in weight will earn a reward and then a step and then two steps. You don't need a perfect leg yield on the first try but eventually need more than a shift of weight. Build the concept slowly.

Practicing new communication skills

So how does all of this work? Let's use the halt as an example of how you could start using these ideas. One of the most misused pieces of equipment is the bit, so using halt as an example of training will allow us to see how to communicate without falling back on a piece of equipment to gain results. The horse's mouth and the bridge of his nose are some of the most sensitive areas on his body. When using reins, whether a bit is in his mouth or not, we must be respectful with our hands at all times. To halt we typically rely heavily on the reins, but that pressure doesn't mean anything to the horse until we teach him what it means. This gives you an opportunity to teach movements with or without the reins. You don't have to rely on your reins at all if you don't want to, though they can be quite useful for clarification.

The reins are a tool that can be one of the hardest to learn to use correctly. It is easier for us to use our dexterous hands than our body, intention, visualization, or energy. However, relying too heavily on the reins can be one of the most damaging things we can do to a horse, so we must teach the horse what the bit means. Even if you have taught him how to yield from pressure it is still a foreign concept to move away from pressure inside his mouth.

Beginner riders should not be given reins until they are balanced in the saddle. They are devices for communication, not handlebars to keep your balance. All new skills including trotting, cantering, and jumping, should first be taught with some kind of hand-hold for balance, followed by learning the skill with no hands at all. Only when the rider is balanced with no reliance on her hands, should she be given the reins. That prevents her from balancing on reins and accidentally hitting the horse in the mouth. The reins should never be used as a sharp correction or punishment whether on purpose or inadvertently. A balanced rider can apply a rein aid by releasing the reins and then picking back up the contact. Creating a space is just as effective, or more effective, than pulling on the horse's mouth.

Start on the ground to teach the horse to stop and turn from the lightest possible touch on the bit. Make sure your horse knows how to lead and halt in hand and then put a bridle on with the reins over his neck. Don't lead him with the bit. Use the reins as you would in the saddle by gently touching one or both reins for turn or halt. Teach him to lower his head and back up from slight pressure on the bit. This exercise will help solidify the concept and helps prepare the horse for working in a frame. On the ground you can use your body language and energy to clarify the meaning of the bit without having to use a lot of pressure. When you get on the horse, your focus, intent, and visualization are your primary cue and your leg and seat is your primary aid. The reins are there for extra guidance, support, and clarification to collect and direct the energy generated in the body

Rushing your horse through foundational learning is a disservice to your horse. Yes, you can use a piece of equipment or failsafe technique to get what you want, but the horse isn't actually learning how to learn. If a child was struggling with the concept of division in math class you wouldn't say "oh well" and give her a calculator. While the child would be getting the answers to the division problems she hasn't learned anything more than how to punch numbers into a calculator. You have not actually taught her to do division. When she gets to work with fractions or algebra later on she will be confused and unable to understand what is happening because she is missing an integral part of the math foundation. Horses are the same way. Learning to halt is an area that I often see taught with a calculator, or in this case, a bit.

Halt is one of the first things you teach. The horse doesn't need to learn how to stop – he already knows how. Rather, the human needs to learn how to communicate her request to stop. The person can help the horse improve his movement under saddle but it is the human that is the true student. Your horse is your guide and teacher as much as you are his. Listen to your horse. Teaching him to halt off your body and intention can be difficult for the rider but if you successfully teach it you have taught your horse to listen to your seat and energy. This becomes the foundation for backing up, working in collection, lateral work, and transitions that you will use later in training.

Common riding and training involves a series of demands. Yank him in the mouth and if he doesn't stop, yank harder. The only reason he stops, if he does stop, is to avoid any more pain. How often do you see riders pulling and pulling for a "whoa"? So many riders get into a tug of war with their horse's mouth, which exerts intense pressure on sensitive structures. When struggling to get a horse to stop or slow down, riders put on a stronger bit and then try a whole series of techniques including the pulley rein, the one rein stop, running the horse into the rail of the arena, or standing in the stirrups as though water skiing on the horse's mouth. That is typically met by resistance from the horse, resulting in a variety of problem horses: the fighters, who resist the process and barely stop; the creepers, who keep slowly moving forward one step at a time; the dancers, who fidget at the halt; the rooters, who try to snatch the reins away from the rider; the evaders, who run inverted with their head up and mouth wide open; and the defiant, who toss their heads in revolt.

When training the halt by relying solely on the bit, the methodology tends to dictate that initially the rider should use any force necessary to get the horse to stop. The next step is to try to get the horse to halt more precisely with softer hands. Going back to the calculator analogy, this is like learning to use the calculator faster and with more accuracy but still not learning long division. The horse hasn't properly learned the skill. When a horse stops because the rider is pulling on his mouth, he is inevitably falling onto his front end and pulling against the rider.

The reality is that a horse can't make a clean stop while on his front end. The best halt is where the horse shifts onto his hind end and stops the forward motion while staying very light in his front end. This doesn't come from the bit but from the rider's body. The exaggerated example is a sliding stop. A good rider doesn't touch her horse's face. She sits deep in the saddle, pushes her legs forward, and elevates the horse up into a stop where the horse sits deeply on his hind end. I'm not suggesting that you need to learn a sliding stop but that you teach the horse to stop by using his hind end.

Often a rider becomes frustrated when trying to stop, slow, or turn without the reins. They have come to rely so heavily on them that they feel out of control when they can't get the horse to do what they want. That problem is on you, the rider. What are the mental blocks that you are facing? What emotions are rising up in you and why? How can you deal with those beliefs and feelings in a positive manner? This is also a chance to use creative problem solving. What do you need to do or change to help your horse understand what you want? When you pull on the bit you are demanding that the horse stops, and if he doesn't, you will relentlessly add more pain until he gives you what you want. When you make that decision you are taking away the horse's right to choose, his freedom, and his power and you put your partnership at risk.

Riding the halt off your seat requires giving the horse a clear message with your energy, intention, and body weight that you would like to stop. The horse then chooses to respond. Ideally, you block his forward energy and he willingly agrees to halt. You can help him by utilizing someone on the ground to block his forward movement to translate what you want in a way he understands. Ask for help. You don't need to be a hero. Remember, horses exist through movement so you must earn trust for your horse to willingly comply with your request.

Visualize the halt, believe in your ability, and feel certain the horse is going to stop. Mirror what you want the horse to do by tucking your pelvis and sitting down in the saddle. Use your weight to shift back and help him balance his weight back and lift his shoulders. Ground your energy and block the horse's forward energy coming through his back. Use the reins as support to block the forward energy by releasing and picking back up the contact.

Use your body, breath, and intention to work with the natural rhythm of the horse. Don't try to control every move he makes. It's about getting him to willingly work with you. Use your body like a metronome to maintain, and then stop, the rhythm of the horse. For example, in a canter your body naturally sinks down into the saddle on the down beat and then raises back out of the tack as the horse shifts his weight from the leading front leg to the hind end for the start of the next stride. It is the point that you naturally rise out of the saddle and swing your upper body forward that the horse rocks onto his hind end. It is when he is on his hind end that he can stop. So, disrupt his rhythm by staying deep in the saddle with your hips forward. That is already your cue to stop and you are asking for "whoa" at the point he can give it to you without pulling on you or falling on his forehand.

Find ways, with intuition, to work within his natural rhythm to get the response you want. Horses will match playmates' strides while playing. Use your body to teach him to match your "stride", rhythm, energy, and intention. If you ride that same point in canter with just a moment of hesitation you have a half halt which will encourage the horse to pause and lift in canter to give you better collection or slow down the pace. If you really stop the energy, which can be done in varying degrees, you can get a transition to trot, walk, or halt. You must be clear, apply the right amount of resistance in your body, and then follow the rhythm of the desired result. Prepare your body through visualization and communicate accordingly. Finding the rhythm and sweet spot for each gait and movement to apply an aid requires feel, timing, balance, and clarity. Use your breath work, awareness, intuition, and visualization to help you.

Work on good halts with an added step backward to solidify the idea and encourage him to tuck his pelvis. Once you start to get the halt you can provide the horse support and encouragement to do it more reliably and shape it into a really nice halt from all of the gaits where the horse ends up standing perfectly still. It is crucial to reward all of the small improvements along the way. As with everything, don't give yourself a timeline. Be patient. Every time you get on you have to work on halt at least once, unless you want to do an emergency dismount, so you literally have the lifetime of the horse to practice. It should not be a tedious drill. Make it interesting by stopping over poles, pairing it with rein back, and having the horse stand for varying lengths of time. Sometimes ask him to stand for a couple minutes and sometimes "kiss" the halt for a second and then ask him to move off. Keep it clear. You don't want the horse to learn to move off without a cue.

Part of the challenge is that you are giving the horse a choice which means he can say "no". You have to accept that and not punish him. You must find a way to make it fun or inspire him to want to work with you without coercion. When you develop a strong partnership your horse will trust you and want to work with you, the flip side is that you must trust your horse and want to work with him, not against him.

The horse doesn't want to do anything repetitively for no reason. So have a purpose when you ask for halt, such as "I would like to look at this view" or "I would like to help you get balanced" or "I would like to get off now". If your horse is struggling with a concept, you can ask him to do something else at which he succeeds. As your halt starts becoming solid you can practice it as a way to reward him and make him feel successful and proud. Halt also has the added benefit of providing a breather to sit and just be before collecting your thoughts and intention to return to the task at hand.

When you teach the horse a better, balanced, more powerful halt, it is beneficial to him. You are also benefitting by learning how to diffuse a situation gracefully, deal with your emotions, and ground your energy. Accomplishing the task makes both of you feel good, builds your confidence, and makes you feel proud and successful. Those feelings are then translated and sent to your horse and the entire experience is more joyful. Remember that the goal, initially, is not a perfect halt. There will be chances to celebrate little things all along the way so use them to raise the energy and excitement for the work that you're doing. The real goal is partnership, trust, compassion, joy, empowerment, communication, and fun. Learning to halt is just another way to work on all of the things that really matter. It's not about the task – it's about you and your horse.

There will be times when you need to fall back on more traditional ways of doing things. Your horse spooks and takes off and you feel unsafe so you use the handy, effective one rein stop to pull him up. Or if your horse becomes overly excited you may need to disengage his hind end to help bring him back down and remain safe to work with. A horse with his head straight in the air is never calm while a horse that is grazing is never on high alert.

There is no need to throw away all of your training and skills – we are just shining a new light on them. Don't take away his power, punish him, or use these techniques in a harsh way. Just redirect him and immediately go back to communicating in a less physical and demanding way. Build back up the trust and understanding. It would be ideal if someday, maybe fifteen years down the line, those things wouldn't be necessary in your partnership but horses are horses and stuff happens. Our safety and that of the horse must come first.

Don't get yourself injured, which will do more to break your trust and confidence, in an effort to be perfect. It is not realistic.

However, you should never use harsh, sharp aids. You shouldn't need to. If your horse is slow off your aids go back to the ground where he can see you or have someone on the ground help you. Look inside yourself for the solutions. This doesn't create a quick fix but it does allow you to build a long-term relationship. The pay offs are well worth it eventually. Training and riding isn't easy. There is a lot going on when you ride so be patient and just keep fixing the areas that aren't working.

Ride off a whisper, not a shout. How effective is shouting at someone to change their mind? They either dig in and defend their position or agree but with resentment. Always understand what you are asking the horse. When you control his movement you control his expression and his life. He is surrendering to you. For example, when you ask a horse to flex at the poll or drop his head you are taking away his control of his sight. He needs to really trust that you will do right by him.

We have a chance to begin collaborating with the horse and working in a way that benefits both parties without the threat of fear or pain. The work itself becomes rewarding for everyone as we find the synergy that allows us to train the horse to the top level of any discipline. In fact, you can reach your goals with the horse and both of you can be more empowered than when you started training. It may take more time, patience, and understanding, but both of you will be better off in the end. The training helps to develop the whole horse, the whole human, and the partnership.

Furthermore, if we can learn to be still and communicate with the horse in this manner we will also learn how to start communicating with the universe. We can learn to manifest our dreams. The law of attraction came into the mainstream as a way to attract our desires into our lives. This concept is really about quieting the mind, doing away with negative and limiting beliefs, holding your intention in your heart, and actually believing in your own power.

Thoughts generate emotion and firings in your body that are all energy and energy attracts like energy. When you use your power to vibrate on a positive level, in tune with your soul, and in service to others, the universe steps up and takes care of you by returning love, fulfillment, happiness, and peace.

Chapter Six:
Humble Leadership

***Humble**: not proud or haughty; not pretentious*
***Leadership**: a process in which one person can enlist the aid and support of others in the accomplishment of a common task*

It is time to step into a leadership role to mold your training sessions and help the horse to develop. In every dance there must be a leader to make the dance fluid and synergistic. The leader must work in collaboration to support her partner and contribute in a positive manner to the expression of the movement. The dance would be incomplete without both partners but one person must hold the space so that both partners remain in step. This does not mean that she shoves her dance partner around the floor dictating every movement. In fact if the leader did that, the dance would end up stiff, rigid, and confused. The dance would lose its beauty and rhythm without a strong, yet compassionate, leader.

The dynamics of leadership

There is a big difference between a boss and a leader. A boss gives orders, makes demands, and wields external power. A leader inspires, guides, and has a quiet assuredness and confidence that causes others to follow her willingly because they sense the inner power in that person. One sees herself as separate or above those under her command and the other sees herself as one of the people she leads. Any person in a position of influence over others, whether it's a manager, priest, teacher, parent, or trainer, has a choice of being a boss or being a leader.

From the perspective of the person being influenced – the employee, parishioner, student, child or animal – which would you prefer? Someone who is separate, insecure, unfair, tyrannical, always right, better than you, demanding, and controlling? Or, someone who is connected, confident, powerful, inspiring, just, kind, fair, honest, humble, who sees you as an equal and allows you to find your way through encouragement? From the perspective of the influencer, how would you rather relate? How does it make you feel to boss people around? Would you rather feel like others want to work with you?

When you use external power to be the boss, everyone loses. The boss gives her true power away and the employee, or horse, has his power stripped. When you use internal, authentic power to lead, everyone gains. The leader grows and flourishes while helping those she leads to do the same. You get a better outcome with a leader than a boss. No one can find well-being, purpose, and joy when in an abusive relationship. Sometimes less is more and you can gain even better results when leading by example as part of the process and part of the team.

A true leader's responsibility is not to herself but for the good of others. A leader is in a position of service to those she leads. The welfare of those she leads is the bottom line. You cannot act in selfish ways for personal gain. Leadership is not a position of privilege. It is a position of the humble servant. You are there to lift others up and to bring action to create something bigger than yourself. As a leader you must have confidence but also act in a just and fair manner. You must be willing to takes risks but also act with humility. You cannot be full of pride and focused on seeking status. A good leader lets others celebrate the successes of the team. The leader acts as a catalyst for the group but is not the only, or even the most, important part of the group. She has one of many titles and it takes the entire team to achieve success.

Becoming a leader is also about your personal growth and development of leadership skills. What beliefs about yourself do you need to let go? What beliefs about your horse are holding you back? How does this partnership mirror other relationships in your life? Is your approach to leading the horse similar to the way you treat your partner, kids, parents, siblings, friends, or coworkers? Can you find a new approach to relating to the horse? Could that new approach carry into other relationships in your life?

Remember that your position has nothing to do with whether you are equal to someone or not. As a parent you have more authority than your children or as an employee you must listen to your manager but you are still equal. You are no better or worse than anyone else. We are all people and a part of spirit, regardless of age, money, skin color, gender, or status. Work with everyone as though they are your equal. Treat everyone in a fair manner.

If you see everyone as equals but understand the level of authority in a situation, it is easier to accept circumstances. You can still have more authority than others at work but be a fair manager who leads and inspires. The relationship you want to build with your horse is an equal partnership. You will be stronger in some areas, and weaker in others, but there is a balance. Neither of you is fully in charge of the other. You are each responsible for yourself and you can act in a manner to support the other in their endeavor to be whole, free, and full of authentic power.

Horses can teach us leadership skills

Horses naturally seek out a leader, or try to become the leader, because without a leader there is chaos and uncertainty in the herd. To become that leader, you must act in a way that your horse chooses to follow. You can make threats and demands and try to force the horse to follow you; or you can be trustworthy, dependable, humble, and act with integrity to truly lead the horse and inspire him. We expect the horse to respect us and listen to us. We even try to demand it.

There is the belief that if we move his feet like an alpha horse then we can make him have respect. We try to always be the one to move the horse's feet and push the horse away until we allow him to join us based on the behavior of the alpha mare in a herd. Our attempts to replicate the horse's behavior can be more damaging than teaching the horse to respect us as a human leader. We will never be able to function or communicate like a horse. Furthermore, to be a true leader in a herd you must live with your horse 24 hours a day.

We cannot replicate the lead mare but we can learn about the qualities of a true alpha to learn leadership skills. You can make the horse submit but you can't force respect. It has to be earned. It is very typical human behavior to want to be respected without first becoming respectful or to want to be trusted without first becoming trustworthy. When you try to demand respect, trust, or obedience you are assuming that you are better than the horse and you are asserting your dominance. You must remember that a horse, or anyone, must choose their leader and decide if you are fit for the job.

Sometimes we have the wrong idea about who is the leader in a herd. The bully that pushes the other horse out of the feed bin is often mistaken as the lead or alpha horse when, in fact, that horse is often just the bully. There is a difference between the bossy mare that makes ugly faces, kicks out, squeals, and pushes everyone around and a lead mare whose presence alone gains respect. Other horses do not necessarily respect or follow the bossy mare. That horse is like the boss who can demand work out of you, or push you off the pile of hay, but that you feel no loyalty toward and, when given the chance, you disengage from her because she disempowers you. The lead mare does not have to exert herself on others. A flip of the nose is enough because she is a true leader with authentic power.

A lead mare is not unjust. She may reprimand a horse but does not punish. She may assert herself to keep the herd safe, keep the peace, and maintain her position but that is the role of a good leader. A lead mare does not needlessly pick on others. She does not just socialize with other alphas or more dominant horses. She simply knows that she has a dominant personality, and as such, follows her purpose of leading the group – a position that comes with perks and disadvantages. The highest ranking horse in a herd will play with and groom the lowest ranking horse. She is not above, or better than, any other member in her herd and she relies on and interacts with all of them.

The lead mare instills confidence and, through persistence and consistency, demonstrates that she can be relied on to keep her herd safe in times of danger and lead the group to resources. All horses will test her because they need to know that they have a trustworthy leader. Some horses, and some humans, are naturally dominant or submissive. So many trainers teach that the horse will constantly try to overthrow you as the leader in your herd of two. This is not necessarily true. Dominant horses may want to be the leader because that is their personality and their calling. More submissive horses may just test you to ensure they can actually rely on you, that you have the characteristics of a leader, that you won't back down, that you have confidence, and that you will make decisions with everyone's best interest in mind.

In addition, a horse and human team is not the same as a herd of horses. In the herd there are many important roles including the lead stallion and the number two and three mares. There are horses who discipline youngsters and those who stand guard. The herd is not controlled by one tyrant nor would the herd be able to function or remain safe without the contributions of all. Each horse applies its strengths for the benefit of the whole. One role within the herd is no better or worse than another. Just as we need school teachers and doctors and sales clerks for our society to function, each horse makes a contribution and plays a different part. Every horse has a voice and, even though there is a hierarchy, each horse's opinion is heard. If the most submissive horse in the herd spooks, the lead mare does not write off the possibility that there is a threat because it came from a low-ranking horse. She relies on feedback from all of the members of the herd and they work as a team. Her job is not to dominate others. The lead mare is not the best horse in the herd; she is just the best leader.

Horses will follow good leadership but it is unwise to think that pushing them around or controlling their every move constitutes leading. You must lead by example and be the change that you want to see in your horse. It is important to set boundaries and be firm and confident. Be clear about your expectations but without attachment or judgment. Following a strong and fair leader makes the horse feel safe. You have to demonstrate that you are a person capable of leading and a person worth following before others will accept you as the leader. That comes from within you and not from superficial actions. You earn respect through consistent and reliable action that is of service to others, authentic, and aligned with your purpose. You can't demand respect. You have to earn it and keep earning it through your actions.

You don't turn to a person who panics in a crisis. You turn to the calm, collected, confident individual who is capable of making decisions under pressure. You must be that person for your horse. When your horse asks if you are worthy of leading you must believe in yourself while remaining grounded enough to listen to the feedback from your horse. Each horse is different. You may be required to play different roles in your partnership depending on the type of leader your horse needs you to be, whether that is to provide confidence or boundaries or motivation, all of which requires you to listen and remain humble on the soul level. You are no better or worse than any other living thing for the essence of every living thing is the same. We are all part of the same spirit. Open your heart, connect from your heart, and lead from your heart. Be a leader that inspires an outcome, not a leader who demands an outcome. Encourage creativity and celebrate your horse's successes.

Methods- and results-based training can thwart the true gifts and wisdom of the horse. Trust the horse's intuition and follow his lead and insight at times and, in turn, lead him at other times. Support one another. As a leader you are not sitting at the top all alone and you do not have to act stoic. You are leading a horse who is, by nature, a teacher. Ask for help and support from the horse. Stay humble and act with humility to accept his support and encourage his ideas.

When horses play or run together in joy they will often fall into perfect sync, their strides lining up together. Through confidence in knowing who they are, the more dominant, faster, stronger horse will not feel threatened by matching the stride of his playmate. He may even let the "lesser" horse get ahead or get in a good nip because the horse knows that the game is about feeling good, not winning or proving himself. The game is not fun if one horse is bullying the other. They mirror each other in the power and grace of expressing who they are. There is no need to show off or prove that they are better.

You can also fall into this type of teamwork through play with the horse without the need to dominate or prove your position of authority. What is left is joyful mirroring. You and the horse both have strengths and vulnerabilities, but that doesn't matter. You can come together anyway. This is a great lesson for employees, parents, or anyone in a position of power. Assert yourself when necessary but don't be afraid to run with your herd and play. Don't isolate yourself on some false pedestal. Fall in sync with others and enjoy their company. Maybe you can even learn from them.

As an equal you still have to stand up for yourself, claim your power, and act with authority. If you are dealing with a super pushy horse then you have to show him – not with more force but with speed and accuracy – that you can't be pushed around. You must deal with each horse as an individual. The confident, pushy horse should not move your feet and make you back down but that doesn't equate to you needing to make the horse submit. Instead, you find a way to show that type of horse that you are equal and worthy of trust and respect. With the frightened, nervous horse you may need to give more space and let him move you on occasion by taking a step back to prove that you are an equal and worthy of trust and respect. It's not about dominating or manipulating the horse to get what you want. It is about leveling the playing field and working together to meet the needs of both parties.

Leadership doesn't mean that you are always right or have the only say. It means that you are the one who starts guiding the process to form the training to reach your goals in your discipline. The horse isn't going to miraculously say "I would like to work on dressage, walking across a wooden bridge, or roping". You will initiate the activities and set the direction of your training but the horse should have input and a voice along the way as your partner. Through leadership, you start to guide and influence the horse which leads to meaningful work that is expressive, harmonious, and joyful. The horse maintains his freedom of movement but you begin to work as one. It takes time and patience to get there.

Teaching your horse to read and write

Don't tell your horse what to do or even ask him to do something. Lead him to the desired outcome and inspire him to greatness. Partnership is never built by making one party weaker. It takes the horse's power away if you train the horse by getting him to do something to avoid pain or fear, and it takes your power away if you train the horse by begging, wishing, and pleading. Partnership is built by leading the horse with positive energy and communicating in a clear and fair manner. Your horse will follow your example if it is done with the right intention. Motivate him to work with you and keep his best interest in mind. Horses will put in a great amount of effort but they expect you, as their leader, to do the same. You can't be daydreaming or lazy. Stay present and strong. You will only get as much as you give.

Be careful of looking at training with the mindset of "How do I get my horse to do X?" or "How do I get my horse to stop doing X?" Instead, ask yourself how to build a relationship to assist the horse in learning so that training a new move is based on strengthening the communication, trust, and respect that you have started to build. Each new step in training is an exercise to obtain your goals of empowering the horse and realizing your dreams while reaping the benefit of learning a new move in the process. To effectively lead, you must be open to creativity but with a strong vision of where you want to go. You must remain open minded in the process, let go of emotional negativity, and inspire each member of the team to find joy and purpose in the work. It is your responsibility as the leader to instill a desire to grow as a team and ensure that your horse can be successful.

Horses are fluent in the spoken language of the horse. Any movement that you ask your horse to perform is something he already does naturally. The horse can carry himself with perfect balance while executing the most technical movements. We do not need to teach the horse how to move. However, we do need to teach the horse how to move under our weight and based on our cues. This is the equivalent of teaching a child who can speak how to read and write. We must take the horse's natural movement and language and translate it into a series of symbols and cues that we can use to build a story. This is similar to teaching the horse to read and write.

Just like with a child, the process of learning the written language must be broken down into logical steps that build on one another into more complex thoughts. It takes a human many years to get to the point that they can write an essay or read a novel. We must allow the horse time to work through the learning curve and become proficient in working in partnership with people. We must break training down into logical lessons that progress naturally through their training. It is important to remember that, like children, each horse will have his own strengths, weaknesses, learning styles, abilities, and interests. You must work at your horse's pace with each new concept and keep in mind that sometimes less is more.

When training the horse you must start with the ABCs as your foundation. This includes haltering, grooming, working on the ground, moving away from pressure, accepting equipment, accepting the rider's weight, and offering responses to stimuli. There are dozens of fundamental pieces that must be learned as a base to training under saddle. I would consider all of these things to be the consonants in the alphabet. They are absolutely integral to forming words and will be put together in varying combinations to create different meanings. If you skip any of the basics, you will eventually come across words or phrases that you cannot build without that letter. It is important to take the time to learn the entire alphabet so that you don't have to send the horse back to kindergarten later in training.

Although consonants make up the majority of the alphabet, the English language is useless without vowels to link the consonants together. Vowels make up less than twenty percent of the alphabet but are present in every single word. They are the power house letters. In the case of teaching horses the fundamentals, vowels are represented by core values such as trust, relationship, respect, confidence, and communication. These core concepts will be utilized, in some combination, in every task you ask your horse to complete. You cannot have solid movements and training without linking your basic training together with solid core values. As you are teaching your horse his ABCs I want you to remember the importance of vowels.

Once your horse knows the alphabet you have all of the building blocks to continue training. You never need other letters. You have the basics and then begin to put those things together into words or more complicated tasks. The next things you would teach a child are short, simple words. These are words that the child already knows but you are teaching her how to read and write the word. For example, one of the first things you will likely teach a horse after you get on is to walk forward. The horse already knows how to walk – he's been doing it since he was less than an hour old. However, it is a new thing to walk forward on command while carrying the rider's weight. This is like learning to spell the word "cat". You take the concepts that you have already taught the horse and put them together to create the desired outcome. Let's say the "c" is the training foundation of carrying your weight and the "t" is moving away from pressure. You have to have a vowel in there so we will call the "a" trust. You combine carrying your weight with moving away from pressure linked together with trust and your horse walks forward off your leg aid.

At this point he deserves a gold star at the top of his paper. Be sure to reward every movement that he correctly gives you. This is not the time to fuss over how fast he walked off, if he went in the correct direction, or how he carries his head. All of that comes with time. You can't be disappointed when your child has messy handwriting, can't yet spell the word "dog", or doesn't understand punctuation. You haven't taught those things yet. Reward the horse for walking forward. When he has practiced that skill, you can try another short word. The rest of it will come with time. You slowly start to teach your horse more basic words and soon your horse will be able to walk, trot, canter, turn, stop, and back up without too much of a struggle because you are using a concrete alphabet the horse understands.

The next logical step is to teach the child really simple sentences such as "the dog ran". You want to start with words they have already learned – keep it short and simple. This will look like basic patterns and transitions in training. Maybe you want the horse to walk a figure eight pattern with a halt each time you come to "x". To do this you use the basic words that the horse has learned – walk, turn and halt. Remember that each of those words is made up of the foundational pieces that create the alphabet. You can't lose sight of the individual letters and simply view it as a word. The letters form the words and the words form the sentence. This also means that you must hold onto those vowels – practice your relationship, communication, trust, respect, and confidence in every section of every ride. It is also important to remember that this is still a simple sentence structure – do not ask for straightness, bend, working in a frame, or perfect tempo.

If your base up until this point is really solid the child will be able to start sounding out words. You can ask for more complex "words" through your aids and the horse should be able to start deciphering your intent based on the aids applied. This is the point that you start to ask for the horse to carry himself correctly, bend, straighten, move laterally, and change speed within each gait.

Remember that these are separate concepts and you must build them in a logical manner. Bend at walk is different than bend at trot or canter, just as working in a frame is different at walk than at trot or canter. If you want the horse to bend while in a frame it is an even more complex word and is, again, different between the gaits. The horse is starting to learn more complex words but being able to write one difficult word does not mean that he will automatically know the next word.

From here you start to build more complex sentences with longer words. Perhaps you go back to the figure eight pattern but now you are asking for straightness, bend, a change of speed within the gait, or a lateral movement within the figure eight. I would recommend learning each of those things one at a time and then slowly combining them until you can have any or all combinations within the same figure eight. You cannot expect to accomplish everything all at once. Allow your horse time to learn one concept, reward him, and then move onto the next concept. Eventually, you get to the point that you can put together entire paragraphs and then full stories.

Remember that a child does not start reading the classics in third grade. They know every single letter in a classic and will even understand a lot of the individual words but they are not yet to the point that they can follow such a complex story. If you ask them to read something that is beyond their ability you will discourage them. The goal is to pick stories that are a challenge and introduce new words or concepts but are not so far out of reach that the child is left feeling stupid. The same is true for horses. You want to push them to learn but you don't want to overwhelm them or punish them for failing to succeed at something that they are not yet ready to accomplish. You must encourage them and reward them for trying hard and never break their spirit. Just because you can read the novel doesn't mean that they are ready to go there with you. You must work with them at their own pace.

It is also a really nice reward for children to get to choose books that they enjoy. Children will choose more challenging books if they are on topics that interest them. Give your horse a chance to read fantasy books if that is what he is into. In other words, go on trail rides, play games, or go back to basics on occasion. No one wants to read text books everyday – it kills your enthusiasm for reading and writing if you never get to enjoy the creative, fanciful side of language. Don't just drill your horse in the ring. Everything you do can be enhanced by changing things up. Even if you do flat work out in a field on occasion you will get better movement and enthusiasm from your horse.

Remember, that even when you get to doctorate level work you are still only working with the same 26 letters in the alphabet. You never move away from that foundation – you just build on it. So take the time to teach the basics and to teach the horse how to learn. Also remember that you can never decide to stop using one of those foundational pieces because then the entire framework of the written language falls apart. It takes years to get to upper level work in any discipline but you must carry each lesson that is learned along the way to be able to build the full story. You can't write the next great American novel without the letter "q" or the word "the" – they are small but integral pieces of the English language.

To accomplish this growth and development you must act as a leader throughout the training process while allowing self-expression for both of you. As you develop your intention the horse will respond to your requests but he still has to have the freedom to choose something different. Accept that at times your horse is right. Be creative and patient to learn how to clearly and kindly teach the horse each new concept. The goal is helping him be a strong, empowered horse not just checking the skill off your to-do list. The horse should remain content, relaxed, and confident in your work together. A good leader asks how those she leads feels about the process. Is it of benefit to all? Does the horse understand what you want? Is the work fair and just? Maintain your compassion and sensitivity throughout training.

Managing misunderstandings

At some point you will come up against some sort of misunderstanding with the horse when training. We are often taught to view misunderstandings with the horse as conflict and blame the horse for misbehaving when, in truth, we are also complicit. As a child I had a fear of jumping and my pony could read my hesitance about making it to the other side of the fence. When he listened to my reservations and refused, my instructor would tell me to "not let him get away with it" or "hit him with your crop and show him whose boss". This didn't address the issue. It taught me to ignore my feelings and punished the pony for listening to my true desires. I was taught the practice of dominance rather than compassion. As we seek to build partnership with horses we must understand and take responsibility for the fact that we play a part in everything that happens to us.

We are always in relation to everything else and the choices that others make have an effect on us. That does not mean that we do not have a choice or a say in the matter and contributed, at least through the way that we filter the information, to the outcome. If you fall off is anyone to blame? Perhaps your horse did something "bad" that caused you to come off but was it not your choice to get on him in the first place? Could you have done more to build partnership that could have prevented that spill? Even if it was the horse's fault we have a choice in how we react to it. Perhaps we need to check the horse for physical problems or discomfort. We can decide to feel like a victim or we can let go of the excuses, grudges, and blame.

When we pick a fight with the horse, he will likely react with equal and opposite pressure. He will fight against you or flee if he has the option. If we stay fluid and rework the issue with patience then we can avoid the tug of war. We have all experienced the horse who pulls like a freight train. We try to resist it but the horse will always out muscle us. The only way to "win" such a struggle is to become harsh and exert fear or pain, which is not an effective way to work together. When you learn to see yourself in others through compassion you can have a different approach to conflict. We have no control over other people or the horse and they will react to circumstances according to their perceptions, beliefs, and insecurities just like we do. We cannot take possession of their work, their stuff.

Conflict gives both of you an opportunity to reflect, see your issues through one another, and read the situation according to the lessons that you need to learn. You can only work on yourself. You have no control over the horse's actions or reactions but you can learn to not take them personally. Let's look at a potential "conflict" with the horse, such as not crossing water. Some of the ways you could approach it would be: determining the horse is disobeying and insisting that he do what you say; becoming angry and lashing out; becoming frustrated and losing your patience; deciding you aren't good enough and giving up; or concluding your horse doesn't respect you. You will likely react in a way that is very familiar to you and that you see in other areas of your life.

This gives you a chance to do two things. First, you can look inside yourself at the underlying beliefs and stories you tell yourself so that you can react to this "conflict" in a different manner. Second, you can look through compassionate eyes and see it from the horse's perspective. Perhaps he is concerned because he can't see his feet in the water, there could be predators, it is a confusing reflective surface, or he doesn't see a reason to take this risk. From there, without taking it personally or becoming defensive, you can keep your cool and get creative to help your horse confront his "stuff", fears, lack of power, or misunderstanding. It gives you the chance to approach the problem in a new light. Changing your perspective will dissolve the conflict. You can stop fighting with the horse and start supporting him. He may still have a long way to go to get to the point that he is at peace with stepping into the water but that's okay – that's his challenge.

The horse is physically stronger but you are more clever. Don't let the horse push your buttons or get under your skin because then you are in a position where you feel threatened and go on the defensive. When you are defensive you will get into a testing match to prove your strength and worthiness. However, if you are a confident leader who knows her power then you can remain vulnerable and compliment the strengths and weaknesses of the horse. When you have inner strength you don't need to prove it or abuse it. You know when to give a little. You can get farther with compromise than competition, but there are times when you need to create boundaries and make your expectations clear. When you stand your ground remain respectful and ensure the horse understands so that you do not cause fear or a breakdown in trust.

To be a good leader you must act like a good leader and be fair to the horse. For example, if you don't know if your horse will cross water then don't go out with a group on a trail ride that will require you to test him. That puts too much pressure on both of you. Always prepare and set him up for success. Also remember to meet his needs and work with his instincts. For example, when you want your horse to relax or work in a frame, you need to look up and be aware of your surroundings because, otherwise, the horse will think that is his responsibility. He will be on the lookout for trouble because instinctually he knows that someone needs to. You must be responsible for your horse.

From this mindset you can support the horse and help lead him through his fear about water by using creative problem solving. Break the issue down into steps. Determine what the issue is and then find the component parts to help him overcome the water crossing. If you think the issue is the actual water then start by working with puddles to get the horse used to getting his feet wet in shallow water. Perhaps you start with just one foot. Or you set up a situation that your horse must move through water to get to his grain and make it part of his daily routine. If you think the issue is stepping onto an unknown surface you can start by asking the horse to step onto plywood, tarps, or other surfaces. If the issue is stepping down the bank into the water, then start by working on hills and ditches without water to build his confidence. Be creative and lead the horse to success.

Shaping the outcome

Change and transformation is a result of reacting to physical, mental, or emotional pressure and without it we would have no reason to grow or improve our circumstance. However, don't restrict the horse so that his only option is cope with the pressure. We don't have to force our agendas on the horse and make him consistently uncomfortable. Pressure is not inherently bad, but there is a big difference between being manipulated or given an ultimatum, and being encouraged and supported to make beneficial changes.

Whenever you work with the horse you apply pressure in the form of your presence or an aid. We use pressure to shape the horse's behavior. While you might not apply aggressive pressure or discomfort, like smacking the horse with a whip for noncompliance, you are still applying passive discomfort to encourage the horse to make a change. It is very important that you give the horse an option to find release from the pressure, not just an option between really uncomfortable and slightly less uncomfortable.

You wouldn't study for an exam or prepare for a meeting without some sort of pressure but that pressure can be negative or positive. If you are told that if you don't study you will fail, never amount to anything, and ruin your life, it will be an incentive to study based on fear. However, if you are told that by studying you can learn something important, achieve a sense of accomplishment, and open doors for opportunities that you deserve in life, it is an incentive to study based on love and hope. Both options may encourage you to take action but one plays on your fears and the other provides you with solutions. Pressure is necessary for change and sometimes you must become uncomfortable in order to do something different.

In a dire situation you might have to apply negative pressure. If a horse is coming over the top of you there is a consequence because it is unsafe and disrespectful. Or if a horse starts running out to a road and could get hurt you may need to use force to handle the situation. However, in the arena when working on half pass or transitions you are not in a dire situation. Take your time and use positive pressure to support the horse. Show him how it will be helpful to learn the task. Training should have deeper meaning and purpose than just saying "If you do this I will stop applying pressure". What does the horse gain from the interaction?

For example, when teaching the horse to rein back, you could approach it as an arbitrary decision or as a means to help him develop. Without a reason for teaching the exercise the only response to the horse questioning the activity is "because I said so," which is not terribly motivating. Instead approach rein back as a trust exercise with the human that can help teach the horse better body awareness and learn to feel where his feet are. That has value for the horse because the horse cannot see where he places his hind feet. He must learn to feel and sense what is behind him in his blind spot. Through teaching this skill you can help the horse and, in the process, build his confidence and the partnership. It also turns into a building block for more advanced moves in the future which is of benefit to you in the training process. Look for new perspectives on how and why you are teaching the horse skills.

Be willing to compromise. I once worked with an unbalanced horse who ran into his canter transitions. He would get heavy, strung out, and fall sloppily into canter. Through a series of exercises I was able to guide him to a balanced transition on his stronger lead where he would step into it with power, grace, and ease. However, the left lead was not as easy. I soon discovered that I could have the correct lead on the left rein and a sloppy transition or a perfect transition on the wrong lead.

Now what? I chose a combination of both. I would ask him to give me the correct lead to build strength in that direction and practiced good transitions going to the right. No worries. We had all the time in the world and did not need perfection right away. Very soon after accepting this I asked for a canter while out cross country. Moving in a straight line he was able to pick up his left lead with perfection. If I had just drilled him in the arena I would not have discovered that I could practice canter transitions out cross country without any problem and that he needed to work on his balance and strength around corners to the left in the arena. Let the process unfold and don't make assumptions.

When training the horse, remember to allow, request, don't take it personally, and practice gratitude. Allow your horse to make mistakes, be himself, and move with freedom and liberty rather than restricting his movement or opinions. Do not assert yourself on him. Then, out of the silence and the freedom you make a request through your intention. It is a suggestion for something that would be of benefit or just plain fun. Remain detached from the outcome regardless of whether you label it as "good" or "bad". Be grateful for his effort, his presence, and the experience. You continue to allow and start the process over. As the horse comes to see that you are not restricting him or dominating him, sees your requests are to his benefit, understands that you will not hold it against him if he makes a mistake, and that you are grateful for him, he will start to willingly participate and try to do what you ask. Then you can begin to guide him and dance with him.

Focus on what is good and not what is bad. If your response to everything is negative then you and the horse will always feel defeated. However, if you can find things to respond to positively, you will both feel enthusiastic. You can typically find something to reward if you are open to it. Be careful of qualifiers. As you start looking for the positive it is tempting to use the "yes, but…" which is annoying and leaves you never feeling good enough. Do not qualify your rewards or your opinions about your work. "Good job bending *but* give me more impulsion." Delete everything after the "but". Reward the bend if that is what you asked for and work on the impulsion separately or your horse will become discouraged.

Try listening to his needs so that you don't get to the point that he is annoyed and has had enough. The horse should never have to look for a reward or relief from work. Bad habits, such as rooting, come from the horse seeking respite. Be a good leader who is quick to let the horse rest and feel good. Take your time with plenty of breaks. A reliable leader does not push the horse too hard or to the point of discomfort. Let him walk on a lose rein if he is hot and blowing or just stand still for a bit. You rarely see people just let their horse relax in the shade for a few minutes. When he is feeling good he will perk back up and ask to start working again. The horse will seek out work if he is not pushed too hard and finds the work itself rewarding. If you ask too much from the horse too quickly you risk over-facing him, but if you don't ask enough he will likely become bored and disinterested.

Considerations for setting up a successful training session

Give yourself and your horse ample time to learn new things. Take off the demand to get it done now, today, or this week. Approach everything as though you would like your horse to learn it in the next few years. Take away the urgency for perfection and it will actually happen faster and easier. Take your ego out of the equation. Work on each task in small increments toward the vision of your end goal without an attachment to the outcome in each individual session. You might work for years to get the perfect 20 meter circle. A lot of riders give the "good enough" stamp of approval on basic moves because they want to move on to more complex concepts, but your foundation is absolutely essential.

Sometimes you can accomplish more by spending less time. Don't sacrifice quality for quantity when training. Practice moderation. Each session with your horse will look like a bell curve or the peak of a mountain. You start slow and build your way up to the peak. There will be small successes along the way but at some point the quality of the work, focus, success, and intensity start to level out. You need to learn to feel for the peak. It is best to end the work at the top or before you reach the top. Try to reduce the frequency of sessions where you fall off the other side and the work starts declining.

You don't always have to reach the peak. If you leave some gas in the tank while the horse still has enthusiasm it will actually motivate him for more. When you push your work too far and it becomes sloppy, or the horse is tired and fed up, or, for that matter, you are tired and fed up, then the team is left weaker than when you began and you are not ending on the best note. Some people start to feel the work go down in quality and get frustrated that they or the horse is not performing as well as they were twenty minutes ago. If you try to push through that it will make it worse because you are still travelling downhill.

The peak for that day may come in twenty minutes or ninety. It all depends on mood, how you're feeling, and what you're working on. Not every day will be as productive as others. Ten minutes of quality work can be enough in a day when you don't feel compelled to complete a task and just want solid progress. Reward the horse for trying. If he only has twenty minutes of good work in him and you planned for an hour, that's okay. Take him for a walk, give him a bath, find something else to work on, or put him away and clean your tack.

There will also be times when you or your horse are just "off". Perhaps one or both of you doesn't have the energy or attention span to work. If that is the case, you don't have to call the horse lazy and push through. The world won't stop turning if you don't work on those canter transitions today. Find a simple task that you know you and your horse can be successful completing, end on a good note, and call it a day. This concept can sometimes be difficult if you only have limited chances to ride or are getting paid to school a horse but at the end of the day the horse's welfare, and yours, should come first.

Horses become bored easily and do not like repetitious drills so break up your training on a regular basis. Always keep your work fresh, new, and playful. Who says that you have to lunge and then ride and then finish? Why can't you get on and off your horse as it seems fitting within a session? Leave the ring and then return, get off and then get back on, or canter before you trot. There are no rules. Challenge both of you by weaving through trees to keep it fun and light. There are endless activities and ways to make training more interesting for both of you if you get creative.

You have to help the horse to build skills and fitness while working on your partnership. Practice skills in fun and inventive ways. Hill work or raised poles will create new challenges and help strengthen the horse's body and build the rider's balance. Help a young horse find confidence, rhythm, and balance by working side by side with an experienced horse that he can mirror. You can also use obstacle courses with tunnels, chutes, and poles to help the horse learn skills like straightness. No one wants to ride a slinky but moving straight is actually an advanced concept because it can be easy for the horse to lose impulsion or fall in or out with the shoulders or haunches.

You must trust the horse to think for himself and give him the freedom to act. Horses don't fall into holes or trip over logs when they are on their own, yet when we ride we feel like we have to watch the ground for them. Let that be their job and responsibility. You don't need to dictate every step and "help" your horse over obstacles. Even when you do more complicated things you can let the horse decide how to handle it. It takes trust, but if you allow the horse to choose his own way he will step up and do the right thing.

I used to ride a mare named Dark Ale who was trained in Ireland as a foxhunter and knew how to think for herself. Coming into a fence all you had to do was plant your hands and stay out of her way. She would trot toward the fence, canter two strides, hit the perfect distance every time, and jump beautifully. If you tried to pick a distance for her and ride her to it, you were in for a rodeo and the most uncoordinated jump ever. She was an independent thinker and, as far as she was concerned, it was not the rider's job to decide where she placed her feet. She had been trained to jump, enjoyed jumping, and was happy to make that decision on her own as an empowered mare.

With freedom of choice comes the freedom to make a mistake without punishment. Expect your horse to do the right thing. The second you doubt your horse, you send mixed messages. Though the intention you put out is for a specific, desired result, do not become annoyed if what you get isn't quite what you had in mind. Reward the effort, stay clear about what you are asking, and continue to calmly work through the problem until it is clear that you have gone as far as you can. With the freedom of choice also comes the possibility that the horse will give you even more than what you asked for. His solution to your request may be a complete surprise in a really good way. Encourage the horse to find solutions that you hadn't thought of and don't limit him. Use different environments, games, techniques, and approaches to see what he comes up with in training.

Ranger is a good example of this. We were out trotting cross country with a group of horses and Ranger and I were bringing up the rear. He was super excited about trotting and a little nervous about being left behind so he started to pull and crowd the horse in front of us. Instead of holding him back, getting into a fight with him, or insisting that he trot a certain way I made a different choice. I chose to trust him, let go of his mouth, and I asked him to do two things for me. First, I requested that he stay balanced over his hind end rather than plowing forward on his forehand, as he had a tendency to do, by helping to balance him with my body.

Second, I requested that he not crowd or pass the horse in front of us by visualizing the space. He, in turn, chose to listen to my requests and came up with his own solution – extended trot. He was not at all to the point that he would be ready for extension as a command in the ring but he felt good and wanted to use his power. He trusted and respected me as a leader so he slowed down and balanced himself, and in the process, discovered extension. I can now build on that trust, feeling, power, skill, and enthusiasm in the future. We both benefit.

Give them space to learn, make mistakes, and react while you stay centered with compassion. Nobody is perfect, yet all are of value. Accept your horse's issues and faults with grace. As we work with the horse it is a give and take. We ride on their backs and share our power and trust. Attitude is everything. You can't necessarily change your circumstance, your horse's behavior, or other people but you can choose how to react to it. We are often surrounded by negativity and take on the same attitude. Instead, ask yourself what you are grateful for, what is working, and what is good about your life. How can you make a problem a solution? When you change your attitude and perception you change your life. What do you want – a positive, happy life or a miserable, negative one?

Horses can teach you how to be a leader in your life and how to live with humility. Remaining true to yourself without letting emotions, self-doubt, negativity, or non-worthiness get in the way gives others room to grow and blossom. Lead without pride or ego to benefit those around you. Leadership through empowerment and loving kindness is not about external awards, it is about internal rewards. Helping others to grow and giving them credit for their accomplishments is of benefit to everyone. It is all about your perceptions and the realization that by giving you receive. Ask the horse for more but respect his opinion. Encourage the best parts of the horse and believe in him and yourself. As you feel pride and joy in your work the horse will sense that and also be filled with a sense of accomplishment and will ask you to lead him to greatness.

Be a leader through life. Give others the freedom to be authentic while supporting their growth and leading them to a higher vibration. Every shift you make to do things differently has a greater impact than just your relationship with your horse. Everyone's actions, thoughts, beliefs, and energy have an effect on the collective consciousness of the universe. You can contribute to raising the consciousness of humanity by approaching your work with the horse in a new light. Take responsibility for your contribution to the whole. Choose to lead through love, compassion, joy, and peace. Live from the heart and lift others up.

Chapter Seven:
Joyful Purpose

Joyful: experiencing happiness that comes from success, good fortune or a sense of well-being
Purpose: the reason for which something is done or created or for which something exists

A joyful, meaningful life full of love is ultimately what everyone is seeking. The path to fulfillment could come from numerous joys including raising children, building your career, connecting to your higher power, finding your soul mate, building community, volunteering, caring for your body, or riding in harmony with your horse. The important thing to discover is your unique purpose, or dharma, that will lead you to the joyful expression of your highest self. In Japan they call it Ikigai, or the reason you get up in the morning. Native American culture refers to your unique gifts, attributes, and attitudes as your original medicine. Do you know what your soul is here to share? Do you know why you get up in the morning? What is your original medicine?

Soulful Horsemanship can give you the skills to not only train your horse but also develop a relationship through which you can unlock a much deeper meaning for you and your horse. It is possible that the work with your horse can help him to fulfill his purpose and express his gifts, which will lead you to unlocking your purpose in life, career, and family. You can lead the horse through his training and he can lead you through your personal development. You can find synchronicity with your horse so that you are both helping the other, enabling you both to give more. You can, through the way of the horse, find greater meaning, joy, and fulfillment in your life.

You have a unique purpose

It is amazing how many people are lost in their lives with no direction. Some are not even aware of what would truly make them happy. We get stuck in negative stories and judgments about ourselves and others. Society teaches us that we will find happiness by seeking wealth, prestige, fame, and recognition, yet most of us have no idea how to obtain that and miss the idea that those things won't actually solve our problems. While those things may provide physical comfort and security, they do more to feed the ego than the soul. External things and validation are always at risk of being lost, which instills fear into our lives. To feed the soul we need internal peace, self-love, and self-worth that no one, and nothing, can take from us.

We will continue to feel as though something is missing in our lives until we embrace who we really are and follow our passion and bliss. That passion is different for everyone but we all share an innate drive for meaning, direction, and purpose. We have a tendency to look outside ourselves to find meaning or our calling. However, your purpose is always calling to you from your heart and is capable of leading you down the path to fulfillment if you listen and take action. Your soul calls to you in your dreams, intuition, and longings. It is there for you to uncover and grasp. Following your passion may not be the easiest road to walk so it takes courage to make that choice. If you can let go of the apprehension, the journey itself becomes rewarding and fulfilling with all of the challenges along the way.

Often the greatest things that we have to bring into the world come through our greatest struggles. It is often out of our weaknesses and vulnerabilities that we learn the greatest lessons and discover the strength of our power. If we can embrace our challenges as being a perfect part of us, and an obstacle to overcome, that will make us stronger so that we can realize our dreams and manifest our purpose. Then we can begin to live in grace and trust the perfection and beauty of the process. Even when things seem difficult and you have hurdles to overcome, you are still learning, creating, and growing. This is what allows you the chance to give birth to the wisdom of your soul's higher calling. Your purpose, your path, is always with you. No one else can provide you with that insight. You must open yourself to knowing your true self without ego's input and then be willing to pursue your calling with a quiet resolve and steadfastness.

When you seek purpose, are you looking for meaning and connection in your life? Or are you looking for recognition and a way to acquire material wealth? True purpose is about service to others and living with humility. If you are seeking recognition then you are still attached to the ego. Ultimately we are all here to serve the greater good by working on our own self-awareness and development. True success is about personal empowerment rather than power over others. Awaken to your inner calling so that you can inspire others to greatness. You don't lose anything when you lift others up and act with generosity. Serve others by giving the gift that your soul is here to give. A purposeful path through life is not inflexible or selfish. Set your soul free by healing the parts of you that are holding you back so that you can give freely of yourself and live a happy life.

You can do great things. You just have to be willing to knock down the walls, jump the hurdles, and climb the mountains that stand between you and your dream. It takes work. Being on the path to fulfill your purpose isn't necessarily easy but the incentive is worth the effort. It is the journey toward that big dream or goal that has the power to change your beliefs about yourself and the world. The real work is walking your path and the real reward comes from the change in your inner state of being. This is also true when you work with the horse – it is about transformation, not a perfectly trained horse. As you change your inner landscape the outer world will begin to shift to stay in alignment with your perspective. You begin to positively sculpt your reality.

Your true work in life has nothing to do with your career and making money. It is to follow a spiritual journey to become aware of yourself; to experience the circumstances of your life; to use your intentions to create your reality; to bring into your life the perceptions, goals and desires that serve your higher self; to discover and live your passion and purpose; to love yourself as part of something bigger; and to recognize your ego as the persona that is attached to your physical body, not a reflection of your soul. Everything is here for a reason, including you. You have been given a unique set of gifts and through your spiritual development you can nurture those gifts to serve the universe. When you find your purpose you find inner knowing, peace, and happiness.

You are a unique puzzle piece. You may have an odd shape or a smooth shape, one color or many, you may be big or small, or an edge or center piece. Whatever your piece of the puzzle looks like it is an integral piece of the overall picture. Without you the picture would have a hole. A lot of people wander through life not knowing where their unique piece fits into the greater picture. They may try to force themselves into a position that doesn't fit. They feel awkward because they have chosen a life that does not lock in properly. In fact, some people don't even know what their piece of the puzzle looks like so they can't even begin to figure out where they might fit.

There are many paths through spiritual practices and science to figure out what your puzzle piece looks like. All religions are different paths to finding the ultimate truth – the essence of spirit within. Whether you believe in the power of the mind, meditation, breath, sound, color, astrology, numerology, Buddhism, Christianity, Hinduism, mother earth, father sky, psychology, metaphysics, horses or any of the other paths to your own truth, you must start with self-awareness. What does your puzzle piece even look like? Who are you? What are your strengths and weaknesses? What are your deepest desires? You must look within and develop reverence for your unique shape and color.

No other piece of the puzzle looks just like you. You are a unique being. Once you know who you truly are – and not just your physical being but who you are on the soul level – then you can go in search of where you belong. To find where you belong in the greater picture you must find the interconnecting pieces that you lock into perfectly, blissfully. You can find your place in the world; the place that you, and only you, are meant to be.

You can't compare yourself to other pieces. They all have their own unique place in the world and are here to fulfill their own destiny. You have your path to follow and cannot walk anyone else's. You were born to fulfill a purpose and to be a small part of the greater whole. You are here to connect to everyone and help to complete the full picture. Your gifts join perfectly with the gifts of everyone else and your place in the puzzle is no better or worse than anyone else's place in the world.

When you find your spot, you have found your purpose and can live in a state of belonging, connectedness, love, peace, comfort, and joy. Every piece is necessary, just as every thread is required to weave a beautiful tapestry. The horse can help you. He can be a mirror for you to examine who you truly are and to help you develop self-awareness. The horse can also guide you to your place in the puzzle. Perhaps he can provide you with the shape that is needed to see how you interlock with everything on earth. Work with the horse can be a journey that leads you to self-actualization if you are ready and willing to step into bigger shoes, into your rightful place in the world.

The horse's purpose

The horse also has a place and purpose on this earth. It is time to stop taking advantage of the horse and, instead, start listening with reverence to the gifts that he brings. You must be willing to respect his wisdom and skills to gain the insight that will uncover your special, unique purpose on this earth. Of all the animals, both wild and domestic, the horse has served humans more than any other. He has a special place in our development and our psyche. He is an important guide, messenger, and teacher. The horse has brought us this far in history. He had gotten us to the point that we no longer rely on his physical strength for our survival. In fact, his true job is just beginning to be recognized. Horses still have much to teach us and show us.

The horse has enabled us to conquer our natural world and one another. He even allowed us to conquer the horse himself. This was a gift that the horse gave to humanity as part of fulfilling his own purpose. There is a reason we were carried on the backs of horses rather than moose or zebras. The horse is special. Think how different our history would be if it were not for this gift. However, that is not the true power of the horse.

I believe horses have endured everything we have asked of them while waiting to fulfill their true purpose in service to the universe. The horse is here to give us power – not authoritative power over others but authentic power and grace. The horse is here to transform and transcend – not the physical world but our spiritual world. The horse is here to inspire freedom – not at the expense of others but the freedom that comes from self-love and peace. The horse is here to help us travel – not to far off lands to wage war but to new realms of understanding and consciousness.

Cultures all over the world throughout history have legends and spiritual teaching that spoke of the horse as a spiritual guide.

Some believe we ride on the horse to this realm or he carries us out of this world when we die. I think horses have the ability to carry us to a deeper understanding of who we are as individuals and spiritual beings. I think humans have always known the horse's purpose but have utilized him for our own selfish gain. That has been the way of human kind. We are now shifting to something greater and the horse is ready to finally start showing us the way. He is ready to show you how to live in peace without being trapped in your own world feeling pressure from others. He is ready to guide you to new perceptions, beliefs, and attitudes. He is ready to carry you into a life of purpose and fulfillment. However, it is up to you, the human, to be open and try a new approach.

If you care to listen and work in partnership with him, the horse can help you reach within yourself and shift from fear to love. It is time for all of us to shift to a new vibration in which each of us, with the support of others, raises our consciousness. It is time to let go of ego-based living in which we live out of fear and in defense of our false identity. It is time to let go of the wars, power struggles, greed, and domination. We have conquered the planet Earth and it is time to start healing and changing our perception. The horse can help you learn to live a heart-driven life based on love, joy, compassion, and peace. He can help you shift from the mind to the soul to manifest your dreams and live in alignment with spirit.

The horse's purpose is much grander than performing movements under saddle. Each individual has his own unique style, identity, personality, and approach to guiding humans. They each have something to teach you. The horse that holds the lesson you need to learn will enter your life when you are ready to learn it. The things you struggle with the most are the lessons your soul needs to learn, so be patient and give the horse the opportunity to guide you through that valuable information. As you work with the horse, it should be reciprocal. You can simultaneously learn from one another. As you teach the horse basic training concepts he can teach you to look within with awareness and align with your higher calling and true nature. It is time for the horse to step into the positive expression of his purpose to guide people to find their authentic power, help people to heal, and to facilitate transcendence.

We are all seeking something more from our lives and, at the core, we are all seeking the same things. Some of those are material things that lead to security and comfort but that is not what will lead you to true happiness. Finding and living your passion is the key. To find your passion you have to strip away all of the negative beliefs about yourself, your fear, the things society tells you, and your self-doubt. The process of working with your horse in a new way, problem solving, and creative thinking can help you work through the layers so that you can see who you truly are. The horse can help you discover your unique gifts, the power within you, and what you have to bring into the world.

Searching for meaning

Awareness leads to awakening. Self-awareness leads to self-actualization. Now is the time to wake up and be present, love wholeheartedly, and have gratitude for every moment you experience. Stop fighting against yourself and others, and stop worrying. Everything will work out perfectly in the end so enjoy the experience. Choose to live for your highest good. We are all perfect the way we are with our faults and blemishes. But, though we are perfect, we are not yet perfected.

A lot of people have a crisis of meaning in their lives even if they are successful by societal standards. If money and accolades are the only factor in deciding what to do for a living, it is likely that you will feel as though something is missing. It is hard to step out of the role of trying to have enough and into a role that fulfills your soul. What will others think of you? Will you make enough money? Will you have security? In the same way that horses begin to thrive when we allow them to utilize their natural skills and abilities, we too can thrive if we align ourselves with our soul's calling, our purpose, and our unique gifts that we have to serve others. This is the true path to belonging but it goes against our culture. Our culture values money and prestige and teaches that it is every man for himself.

We become so attached to our identity, story, and ego that it is hard to surrender and let go of that. We worry that we will be lost without the defense mechanisms and labels. As you become spiritually aligned, your life and your experiences begin to make more sense within the greater picture. You will begin to see that the circumstances of your life, and the individuals in your life, are not random. They are messages and universal guidance provided to help you walk your path. Everything, the good and the bad, begins to become clearer when you surrender to the knowing that we are all powerful expressions of God and that we have a greater purpose then just getting by. Everyday problems that we obsess over are nothing compared to what we are really here for. In fact, the problems we face are actually hidden opportunities. The challenges in our lives serve to guide us to becoming realized humans. The external expression of our lives is there as a catalyst to accepting who we are and can assist us as we work on becoming who we can be.

If you were to suddenly get amnesia you would no longer be who you thought you were. The memories of your life and the stories that you used to base your identity and personality on would be gone. The labels that you had assigned yourself would be gone. So, then, what is left? Who are you at the core? What would happen if you made the conscious choice to let go of those stories and put down your baggage? Who could you become if you let go of all of the things that hold you back? What if you let go of all of the things you arbitrarily decided you weren't good enough for or couldn't do? What would happen if you released your fear and forgave all of the people who harmed you – including yourself?

If you let go of your attachment to your identity then you would be left to live from the heart and realize your true power. Embrace your truth by delving into the heart and listening to the truth it speaks. That honesty is your higher self communicating with you. If you are not your persona, name, identity, looks, or career, then who are you? Don't look to your body or the circumstances of your life when you search for who you are. You must go deeper. You are not your body. You are whatever force is animating your body. You are energy and part of God. That is your connection to the eternal.

We do not take our body and ego with us when we leave the physical world. The ego creates the persona that labels our physical existence but it does not address our essence. Our soul, and the spirit within us, is the piece that carries forward into the unknown. Therefore, the work, development, and lessons learned that deal with the heart space are so valuable to leading a beautiful life in this realm and the next. The actions we take from the heart are valuable to the whole of the universe. The heart lessons are soul lessons that help us along our journey that is beyond this physical form. It is also the heart that connects us through vibrations that we emanate to everyone else on the globe.

However, recognition alone cannot be the only driver behind our work. True interconnectedness is based in the heart space which is where the wisdom of spirit and the collective consciousness lives within us. The mind is a powerful tool but it should not be the center of our lives. The mind does not provide us with our purpose or our authentic self – the heart does. From the heart we are all one. Therefore, serving others is really an act of self-love because you are serving yourself. With the horse as your mirror, you can discover the beliefs, thoughts, feelings, ideas, and emotions that make your heart sing. That is the path to follow because then you are living a congruent life that is on purpose and has meaning. By listening to your inner self you find the outer expressions that make you deeply happy.

If we all have our place in the universe, and a purpose larger than acquiring material worth and looking good, then what is holding us back? A fear-based attachment to the ego prevents us from stepping into the power of our lives. Biologically we have fear of death, isolation, abandonment, and rejection. The same is true for the horse because we are animals and rely on connection and community for survival. We fear taking risks because it is scary to step out on your own. What if you are rejected? What if you fail and can't meet your basic needs? This fear is necessary on an instinctual level to keep our physical bodies alive, but it prevents us from following the heart, living on purpose, taking risks, and being true to the nature of the soul.

Fear manifests into negative self-talk, personal judgment, insecurity, and self-doubt. "I'm not good enough." "People won't get me." "They will laugh at me." "What if I'm wrong?" "What if I fail?" All of this negative internal dialogue makes you powerless and prevents you from living the best life possible. We are so scared of being judged by others. "What will they think?" So we try to either prove ourselves or make ourselves small and unnoticeable. We worry about our appearance, success, and financial status in such a way that we make major decisions in our lives based on how we think others will perceive us. It is even scarier if we are presenting our authentic selves. We become insecure in our own power but we must remember that others should not dictate the course of our lives. Only you can live your life.

Learning to live with power and authenticity will lead you to a love-based life rather than a fear-based life. Your light will shine through and other people will see that and think to themselves that you have something great and wish they could be that happy. You can lead by example. If fear, finances, worry, or negative thoughts and beliefs were to have no impact on you, who would you be? What would you do? Without competition, jealousy, lack of worth, greed, or insecurity, who would you become? If you follow your heart instead of your head, what path would you take? Those who feel that there is never enough in life need to dig down and find out what fear or beliefs are holding them back. Life can be greater than you ever imagined if don't limit yourself. Anything and everything is possible and there is plenty of success in the world for everyone. Life is too short for "what if?"

We come into peace by doing what we feel we have to do, stepping into our genius, listening to the inspired voice within, and following our passion. To hear that calling you have to tune into your intuition and listen to what your heart is telling you to love. If you don't tap into that internal power and follow the calling of your soul, you will be left feeling empty, frustrated, angry, or depressed. You have to follow your intuition moment by moment for it to lead you to a life of inspiration and bliss.

God/Source/Spirit/Life Energy is not out there somewhere. Look within. Look into your heart. That is where the divine lives and is always available. If you listen, your soul will connect with you through your emotions and awareness. Opening and listening to the heart leads to your intuition and creativity. If you can learn to listen to that instead of the chatter in your mind, it can lead you to an understanding of who you are and what you are here to really learn. The horse can show you when you are congruent, aligned, and speaking from a place larger than your ego, attachment to the physical form, and based on societal ideals. The horse can help you uncover the truth about what you think versus what you really feel. He can help you uncover the truth about what you want most out of life.

The expression of purpose through partnership

Let's review the major concepts covered in Soulful Horsemanship to reveal how they specifically relate to finding greater depth in life, joyful expression, and clarity of meaning. The purpose of Soulful Horsemanship is to empower your horse so that he can support you in working through the barriers that prevent *you* from becoming empowered. The horse can lead you to a more enlightened life to express the gifts of your soul. Your horse's eyes are not like a crystal ball that you can gaze upon to find, and know, your destiny. However, the horse can help you find purpose, or your calling, by teaching you how to quiet the mind, look inside yourself for answers, become attuned with your emotions, act authentically, listen to your intuition, develop the power of intention, trust yourself, and examine your strengths and vulnerabilities.

The horse can help you uncover your original medicine by reflecting your soul's desires back to you. He can show you when you are acting in a congruent manner, when your desires and intentions are coming from a true place, what you are most passionate about, and what skills and strengths you possess. The horse not only helps you become emotionally aware, but can also help you integrate both sides of the brain. We shut down the full capacity of our minds, particularly the gifts of the right brain. As we develop intuition and emotional intelligence we begin to strengthen the right side. This also enables us to connect with feminine energy, which we have all been blocking in our society. I think that one reason many little girls are drawn to the horse is through a search for authentic feminine wisdom that is stifled in our society. We are beginning to shift into more balance between the feminine and the masculine and, again, the horse has the ability to facilitate that change.

Working with horses integrates the body, mind, and soul. It can be a holistic way to awaken and integrate your entire body. Riding is a bit like a martial art, dancing, or playing a musical instrument in which you must learn to channel your energy, work in the moment, and strengthen your weaker side. All of these are paths to exploring your true self, developing authentic power, and unlocking emotional freedom. Learning to use the right and left sides of your body independently can help your brain make new connections and open up your creativity and full potential as a human. Working with the horse has the added benefit of the contribution of their love, energy, insight, and wisdom. If you give your horse the opportunity to work with you as an equal, he can help raise you up to new ways to live, learn, and love.

The horse can teach you how to connect from your heart and live from that space. The heart communicates the vibration of your soul, your feelings, and your authentic being. The horse has a profound ability to read that energy. His electromagnetic field, generated by his heart, is much stronger than the human's so he is very sensitive to energy. The horse also emits his feelings from his heart space and can have a positive impact on your energy when you are in his presence. If you are living in alignment with your purpose, your heart will send out the vibration of love, joy, gratitude, and peace. This energy has a positive impact on everyone and everything and carries a stronger energy than negative emotions. You can have a positive impact on others through the vibration of love and healing, which will also affect the horse when you ride and train from this space.

Living in a state of congruence allows you to align the desires of your heart and soul with your physical expression to manifest your authentic power and purpose. When you think about what you want in life, you have to really feel it. Your emotions must be in alignment with your desires. You have to have that burning desire to achieve your dreams or they will remain empty wishes. Emotions are what put out the strong energetic signal to the universe to attract that which you feel most strongly about. If you put strong emotion behind your fear, and not your love, you will be stuck in a state of fear. If you make a career or family choice based on what you think you should do without the underlying emotion that tells you that your heart and soul are on board, then you don't have the power necessary to embrace that decision. If your heart does not say that your decision is a path to happiness and feeling good then the outcome of that choice will never actually make you happy. It can't.

As you become aligned and congruent, your true essence will come to the surface. As it does you must embrace it and take action to do whatever it is. Be the best at who you are. The horse listens to your inner longings and deepest desires. He does not connect with who you think you are or who you think you should be. He responds to the truth of your inner calling. If you do not trust your own wisdom, you can allow the horse to reflect and respond to what you are projecting to provide you with feedback. As you work with the horse ask yourself: What is my legacy? How do I want to be remembered? What do I want? What do I love? What am I passionate about? The horse will respond differently if you answer with your head versus your heart. He can help you separate the truth and wisdom in your heart from the compulsion and desires in your mind.

The things that you are most passionate about are sign posts to your soul's purpose and a life of meaning. Passion for your work is not what you *think* you *should* do; it's what you *feel* you *must* do. It is through knowing and trusting yourself that you can begin to live in a state that you know that you are worthy. You can shift from grasping for more and trying to control the external things in life to accepting the entire truth of who you are and cultivating your inner world. That change in perception leads to an ability to contribute to the world and help others through your actions and your energy. Your passion leads to a life of joy and love.

Compulsive behavior, on the other hand, is fear-based. Compulsion is about all of the "shoulds" and "shouldn'ts" that we feel based on a reaction to the outer world, trying to prove yourself, trying to have enough, and trying to feel safe and confident. When you live in a compulsive state of fear you are avoiding your emotions and your inner world. When you are in this state you will never feel whole. We spend a lot of time looking outside of ourselves in search of something that will heal our inner world but we have it backward. Through healing your inner world you can let your light shine to help change your external world in a positive manner.

You must be careful that work with your horse is based on passion instead of compulsion. The relationship with the horse can be something that you do as part of your identity or as an aversion from your inner world. The barn can become a place where you label yourself as an expert equestrian and hide from the rest of your life. This is the state in which you need to prove yourself, succeed in the show ring, and demonstrate your skill and knowledge.

It is through fear and compulsion that you may begin to manipulate the horse, your external experience with him, to try to find peace and wholeness on the inside. The folks who work with horses in this manner often feel like something is missing. They strive for a relationship with the horse because they want to feel good and fill a hole in their life. When they can't figure it out, they follow the teachings and techniques of others, desperately trying to find the answers from someone else. However, the answers are within. Partnership with the horse is not about the activity fixing you. It is about healing one another and doing the work necessary so that internal change is manifested in the performance of the horse. If you approach the horse with passion and joy, you can look within yourself to listen to and adjust your internal state.

If you can help the horse fall into the vibration of love, instead of fear, not only will he get more fulfillment out of life but he will surround you in an essence that will empower you to grow, learn, and heal so that you can also find more fulfillment in your life and partnership with the horse. The heart is the compass of the soul and it sends your mind and body information through your emotions and feelings. Once you clean up the chatter in your mind you can become aware of what is happening in your body. In the stillness you can hear the messages your heart is sending to your conscious mind. With that awareness, your soul can guide you to live the life that you are here to live. You have the power to embrace your purpose which will make the heart happy. You can live in a different state, free from the stresses that come from being out of alignment with who you really are and what you are here to accomplish.

In order for the horse to walk you through this process you must simultaneously bring more freedom and joy to your horse. Training itself can become empowering for the horse if it is approached with compassion and understanding. Learning to carry a rider, discovering a new way of communicating through sensing the rider, and exploring ways to carry and express himself in a new meaningful manner can all bring purpose in training for the horse.

Riding also has the potential to satisfy the horse's desire to experience adventure, travel, and exploration outside fences or walls which the horse naturally craves.

Part of being connected and part of community is to serve and feel useful. The same is true for the horse. The horse must play a role that is aligned with his strengths rather than just accomplishing tasks for humans. There is a desire to feel valued and recognized for our work. In the same way that we need others to acknowledge our good points and the areas in which we succeed, the horse also needs this sort of positive reinforcement and reward.

As the horse learns to use his body correctly, with balance, impulsion, collection, and cadence, he becomes empowered. His movements become more expressive. It is so much more fun to ride and he, too, feels good about the work and will start to enjoy training and want more. However, the power created when the horse works in this manner relies on much more energy, which the horse naturally wants to conserve in case of danger. The horse does not want to exert himself for no reason as it could cost him his life. Therefore, it is a symbol of trust, respect, security, and comfort if the horse works with you with such power and grace. It is a gift. We cannot demand that he share his energy nor can we take it from him. We must support him in discovering that feeling and then share it with him. This is the feeling that all riders are truly seeking. When you ride in harmony and find oneness, it touches the soul and anything is possible.

You must lead the horse through training to help him be whole, which will result in true movement. To the untrained, unaware eye, top level horses all seem to have this magnificence about them. However, as you become more aware you will begin to see that some horses are working from a state of submission and not freedom. Perhaps the horse's eye is a bit dull, their nose is tight, their tail is swishing, or their movement is slightly rigid. All of those are subtle signs of resistance or discomfort. On the other hand, some horses seem to be dancing in harmony with the rider, joyful, powerful, and floating on air. Two horses can perform the same movement with the same level of technical competency and, while both are impressive, it is the authentically empowered horse that captivates your attention with the magnitude of his expression.

If you recognize that all of the horse's movements, and all of your own, are physical expressions of internal energy and emotions, it becomes easy to see that true collection and impulsion are about an internal state. The outer expression comes from a feeling of freedom and power. It is a physical expression of positive energy generated by a congruent state. To achieve collection, impulsion, elevation, and power you must inspire the horse to greatness and encourage him to feel good about his life. An unbalanced horse that is disempowered, heavy on the forehand, and gives a lackluster performance is also reflecting an internal state. When you dominate the horse and try to force these concepts the horse is unable to find his power, purpose, freedom of movement, and expression. A physically unbalanced horse is a sign of an emotionally unbalanced horse.

Living with authentic power is not about pleasing others. It is about living in service to others based on your passion and talents. When you try to please people, you are simply trying to prevent displeasure in those people and, as a result, act in a way that denies your needs and isn't pleasurable to you. If you deny yourself for the sake of others you will live in a constant state of anxiety that others are not happy. You are not responsible for anyone else's happiness. When you try to take on that role and worry about being judged, your focus is on their experience rather than your own. If, instead, you focus on loving yourself and following your bliss, your resulting actions will support others through your own power. This is a much more effective way of living. You no longer need to worry about pleasing people to gain their approval and admiration because you already approve of and admire yourself.

When you embrace your power you are able to heal yourself and others. You become inspired, creative, and intuitive. You know that you are worthy and deserving of your life. You begin to love others with new depth and meaning. You feel connected to the earth, and everything and everyone on it. You see yourself as part of the big picture. You are grateful for everything, good and bad, because it is all here to teach you and guide you. You have a fire burning inside you. You feel connection rather than isolation. You feel responsible for manifesting your gifts and talents to share with others. You don't have to feel empty or at odds with others. You no longer question the point of life. If you surrender and listen to yourself you can transform your life.

You can simultaneously transform the horse. For example, the center of a lunging circle or round pen is where you can center yourself and your goals. You can support the horse in learning to engage his hind end and teach him how to collect on the circle around you which gives the horse physical and emotional power. To inspire the horse to work with you requires you to turn within and, as you give life and meaning to your intentions, the horse will respond. As his authentic power grows he can support you in uncovering your own authentic power.

When you are in line with what you truly desire, when you are on purpose, and when you have passion, the horse will reflect back to you a mirror of the direction you are heading in your life. If you only want something for superficial reasons, without true passion and meaning, the horse will not respond and your request will not resonate with him. There is a big difference between what the ego wants and what the soul intends. Your outer story or persona must match your inner drive and passion to remain congruent and have the horse respond in a powerful way. The horse can teach you to trust the universe and yourself.

When you shift your focus with the horse, and in life, it can open the door to outer success and allow you to appreciate and enjoy the success you have already created. Working with the horse gives you a classroom to work on shifting from fear to love, control to surrender, and outer to inner. It is an opportunity to experience how spiritual principles work so that you can learn to trust the process and start to make changes in your life that lead to bliss, love, and peace. The horse allows you to experience the interconnection of all things. You will eventually come to see that the successes you have are so much more attainable and rich if you approach them by building connection and sharing with community rather than isolating yourself and hoarding your achievements. It allows you to see that through giving you can receive, and vice versa, because they are one and the same. You are part of the web of life and must find your place within the balancing act of the universe.

Our strengths and weakness can play out in a positive or negative form in our lives. We can express our purpose and calling in a manner that is selfish or in a manner that is in service to others. Sometimes you have to let go of the bad things in order to hang on to the good. It's a choice. As you develop your authentic power you may feel resistance or pressure to stay in your old ways of thinking and acting. This may come from yourself or others. Your ego may kick into overdrive as you let go of your negative beliefs, as ego does not want to lose the identity, story, or persona. The repetitious thoughts of fear, lack of self-worth, lack of confidence, failure, and self-loathing may grow stronger before they start to die down. You may feel defensive of your old beliefs because you are attached to the history and memories. It can be scarier to step into your authentic power than remain in your old, known, practiced patterns.

In addition, those around you may resist your change. As you grow, come into your true nature, and live with positive energy, it can be threatening to those who see your power reflected within them. That is their fear and insecurity. Do not keep yourself small for the sake of others. You can't stop evolving so that others feel better about themselves. Lead by example and show them what can happen if you are willing to take the risk and live the life of your dreams. We all deserve to be fulfilled and to live purposefully. It takes courage to change your life from a state of surviving to one in which you truly thrive. It takes faith to choose to live from the heart. It takes strength to walk your path. If you accept the challenge it can set you free.

Do your life's work. What do you have to bring into the world? What makes you special? Don't hold onto your gifts. Allow the possibilities that are dormant within you to awaken and guide you to a life better than you could have imagined. Let go of the excuses. Stop delaying or waiting for some day when you know more, feel confident, or have the money. You don't have to wait to be happy. Go there now. It is available to you in this moment when you choose to surrender and allow yourself to arrive in your own innermost being. You are enough. Own the beauty within you and set your spirit free. Unlock self-love by finding your deepest joy and connection. Sink into that and feel your connection to all that is. Live authentically. Believe in, honor, and value yourself. Find your voice by speaking to your horse. He won't judge you but he will show you that which vibrates the truth and that which does not.

Conclusion

The work with the horse happens in the heart and soul. Then, as you change, it will be reflected in your partnership and the "shoulds" and "shouldn'ts" melt away. You can simply express your bliss and enjoy the experience wherever it takes you. You then ride with passion, find unity with the horse, and your hearts vibrate at the same frequency. We are not our thoughts or our emotions, but if we listen to the heart it can show us who we are. Through that awareness we can shift the focus from what we do for a living to how we live and who we are. Horses respond to who you are, not what you think you are or what you think you deserve.

The true purpose in riding is not winning awards, just as true purpose in life is not about external things and accolades. Traditionally, one of the major reasons behind training horses has been to win at competitions. Horses get nothing out of winning competitions and neither does the soul. The desire to win is ego-based. Blue ribbons are not the goal; partnership is the goal and blue ribbons are the side effect. Whether you enjoy competition, trail riding, or anything else, the activity will be enhanced by a strong partnership between you and the horse. Soulful Horsemanship is relationship-based work that should be less serious and demanding. It is about the process and the connection. Competition can become a game as a way to continue the inner work, confidence, awareness, and communication between the horse and rider. If you focus on your core skills and personal development you will transcend the normal experience and take your riding to the next level.

When you work with the horse with the goal of creating relationships rather than conquering goals, you can shift your perspective in life. When you learn to face your fears and, in spite of the fear, do what is in the best interest of the horse, you learn to break down the walls that keep you separated and isolated. Life is not about the better job, house, or flat screen television, nor is it about finding a perfect spouse to validate your worth. Life is about the experience. It is about connecting with others. It is about spiritual development and self-awareness. It is hard to face your fears, let go of the external desires, and deconstruct the walls that you built to keep you safe. It is only working through that process that you will truly feel successful and fulfilled. It is through letting go of attachment to the external circumstances in your life that you can find inner peace and come into alignment with the things that your soul desires. It is through vulnerability that you find security.

Don't spend your life asleep without taking risks or chances. Do what you were born to do. Work with the horse in a way that enlightens you. There is enough success for everyone. Luckily we all want different things, are attracted to different people, and have different talents to contribute to the world. Do not get stuck comparing yourself to other's success. Celebrate who you are and your unique soul. Love yourself for who you are and find your power. You don't have to worry about the future because you will trust yourself to make the right decisions.

When you shift to the vibration of love and living in the positive form of your expression you will discover unlimited potential. Positive energy and good things can only flow to you if you are willing and able to give what you have. You must also be accepting of help to revitalize yourself so that you are able to release your power into the world and work in cooperation with the universe and the horse. The horse can give you immediate feedback in learning what that means. Create, imagine, and dream in the arena. Approach the horse with a deeper meaning for both of you. Lead one another to empowerment, connection, expression, joy, love, and peace. Center yourself and find the inspiration to be the person that you are capable of becoming.

Allow the horse to walk with you through this journey of self-discovery.

Working through this process leaves you with a new enlightened outlook. Take a look back over everything you accomplished. How are the lives of you and your horse better than when you started? How can you apply all of these lessons to your life? What have you taught each other? What is the benefit? In what ways can you use these concepts to live a more fulfilling life? How can it help you to be a better person, more effective at work, and improve your other relationships? You can achieve greatness in the arena and have a wonderfully trained horse by working in this manner, but the deeper connection has a greater impact on your life than just developing a riding partner. You now have a soul partner.

ABOUT THE AUTHOR

Stef Durham lives in Central Oregon where she is following her heart to live and work with passion and purpose. Since publishing the first edition of Soulful Horsemanship, Stef married the love of her life and has continued to create meaningful resources for the equine community and beyond.

If you are interested in diving deeper into the concepts discussed in Soulful Horsemanship, visit **www.soulfulyou.com** to join Stef on *A Journey through the Heart with Horses,* a series of heart reflections based on the chapters of this book.

Stef envisions her business, Living Soulful, to become a leading example of heart-centered prosperity and to act as a catalyst for a world in which each and every person knows his/her own purpose. Be sure to sign up to receive updates about future books, classes, and workshops dedicated to the art of Living Soulful.

We are all in this together – as I teach, so do I learn. You are my teacher and my student. The horse is our teacher and our student. I invite you to walk a spiritual path with me and open a space in your heart to allow the horse to be our guide. I love you all and wish you many blessings.

Namaste,

Stef

Printed in Great Britain
by Amazon